SPIRITUAL WISDOM
FOR A PLANET IN PERIL

PREPARING FOR 2012 AND BEYOND

SPIRITUAL WISDOM FOR A PLANET IN PERIL

PREPARING FOR 2012 AND BEYOND

LAURA DUNHAM

Langdon Street Press

Langdon Street Press
212 3rd Avenue North, Suite 570
Minneapolis, MN 55401
612.455.2293
www.langdonstreetpress.com

ISBN - 1-934938-21-1
ISBN - 978-1-934938-21-8
LCCN - 2008935643

Book sales for North America and international:
Itasca Books, 3501 Highway 100 South, Suite 220
Minneapolis, MN 55416
Phone: 952.345.4488 (toll free 1.800.901.3480)
Fax: 952.920.0541; email to orders@itascabooks.com

Cover Design by Jennifer Wheeler
Typeset by Peggy LeTrent

The cover photograph was taken by the author in Northern Ireland in 2005.

Printed in the United States of America

TABLE OF CONTENTS

ACKNOWLEDGMENTS

To the dedicated spiritual teachers, healers, and companions with whom I have shared the path leading to 2012 and beyond, I am grateful for your wisdom, creativity, and support.

To my daily companions, Alden and Tom, who, despite my endless travel and work schedule, offer constant love and laughter, thanks are not enough. Love you, guys, with all my heart.

INTRODUCTION

Why This Book

As I began this book in December, 2007, during the week former U.S. Vice President Al Gore won the Nobel Peace Prize for raising the alarm about global climate change, the world was five years and counting from a key date: December 21, 2012. Expected by millions to mark the completion of cosmic cycles and usher in a new Golden Age predicted throughout human history, Winter Solstice of 2012 is now just around the corner. Will this long anticipated date signal the tipping point of a monumental shift in human consciousness toward enlightenment or the beginning of the end for most species on the planet, including the human?

Which outcome we experience is increasingly up to us. A continuation of life as we know it is perhaps the least probable outcome. The transformation of our world in one direction or another seems inevitable, and we must begin now to direct our intentions and actions toward supporting the highest good for ourselves and our planet. Our choices will have an immense impact on our common future.

Shall we anticipate a time of global peace, an outpouring of love, gratitude, and creativity from a spiritually mature human species living in harmony with the natural order? Or will 2012 launch an era punctuated by global disasters and traumatic change: water and food wars, famine and scarcity leading to massive death and migration, pandemics, drastic climate and Earth changes, worldwide economic collapse, the breakdown of systems of government, religion, and education? Both of these scenarios are possible. Which is more probable? What other scenarios might we anticipate?

2012 is Coming!

An exploration of what lies ahead forms Part I of this book, 2012 is Coming! Signs of the times, prophecies and predictions, possible and probable scenarios are drawn from many sources, some commonly known, others less familiar. This book is aimed at a wide audience, especially those who seek to support the most hopeful vision of the coming transformation of our world. You are likely to encounter material which will challenge your own views and experiences of reality. I encourage you to keep open minds and hearts while exploring this new territory for what it will yield of value to you. What I present is based on years of spiritual and metaphysical study and experience, and I promise you an interesting ride! The human consciousness of the future will need to emerge into a higher harmonic, in concert with dimensions of which most of us are only partially aware. Your discovery and exploration of other realms of consciousness will be a significant part of your adventure and preparation for 2012 and beyond.

Prepare for the Great Shift

Part II, Prepare for the Great Shift, is your guide to participating actively in the coming transformation of life on Planet Earth. It begins with envisioning the kind of world you'd like to live in, gives priority to your spiritual connection, and helps you prepare for the kinds of significant challenges you may face as the world changes around you. Practical suggestions for creating more fulfilling and sustainable lifestyles in harmony with the Earth abound in this section. Ways to develop your own action plan and widen the conversation about what lies ahead complete Part II. An extensive list of resources is also provided in an appendix.

While December 21, 2012 is an actual date, it is also meta-phorical, signaling a transition into a world beyond the limits of time and space. Whether a grand, definitive event happens precisely on that day or we experience transformation in some other way at another time, the Great Shift is coming, and we must prepare. If we approach this transformational era with a sense of adventure rather than with fear, we will be amazed at the opportunities we have been given to co-create a world, indeed, a universe, that is life-giving in all dimensions. What an exciting time to be alive!

Sharing My Journey

My hope is that my own journey along the path to higher conscious-ness will help illuminate your path as well. For the past three years I have felt nudged to write a book that would support the greatest shift in consciousness the world has ever seen. I made several starts and stops. For reasons I now understand, these early efforts fizzled. The book I was supposed to write is the one you're reading now. These three years have blown open my own doors to understanding and connecting with a multidimensional universe so incredibly beautiful and profound that words cannot express its magnitude or meaning. I traveled the planet and encountered energies which are expressions of unseen worlds. Working with these energies and learning how to offer healing to people, places and the planet took me well beyond the academic and spiritual training for ministry I completed fifteen years ago. Now I'm ready to share what I have learned with a wide audience of readers in the hope that you will be encouraged to shift into a higher consciousness for your own sake and that of the planet. Never have the stakes been so high. Changes are coming more rapidly than ever before. It is time—past time—for as many of us as possible to be prepared for what lies ahead on the path to 2012 and beyond.

If you are reading this book, you probably are aware already that the Great Shift, as many are calling it, is underway. A significant number of us have at least begun to anticipate and consciously to create the kind of world we want to live in and leave for future generations. A critical mass of people around the world is waking up, connecting with spiritual Source energy, and from that connection radiating thoughts and intentions that are accelerating the demise of old paradigms and giving birth to a new way of being in a world that works for all. By all I mean not only humans but also Planet Earth herself, our Mother, and the life she supports. We are awakening just in time. For many reasons, Earth and her life forms are in peril, as I will explain in the first chapter, and the choices we make now will determine to a critical extent our common future.

If you long for a peaceful world, where people live in harmony with Earth and all her species, where abundance flows and humanity is free to express its higher order creativity and love, then this book is for you. My intention and spiritual guidance is to help you move with confidence and great hope into a new reality you will help create.

The Great Shift will involve not only a transformation of consciousness, although that is essential, but also in life as we know it on Planet Earth. Earth is the universal Mother who nurtures and sustains us. She is undergoing significant changes, some based on natural cycles that happen periodically over eons of time, and others caused by human action or inaction. These may take the form of extreme events, such as earthquakes and tsunamis, volcanic eruptions, hurricanes and floods, severe drought, increased solar flares and electromagnetic disruptions, even a pole shift, or may be milder and cause less destruction and loss of life–or both. These occurrences have already begun, and we'll explore their impact in detail.

In addition, massive systemic change is underway, involving structures within which we have been obliged to live for centuries. The old paradigm forms of religion, government, nationalism, education, science, economics, health care, social strata, along with linear time and thinking, are giving way to the consciousness of a holistic universe. There is much to look forward to and celebrate as this higher consciousness takes hold. However, the old forms and structures will not necessarily give way easily. We may be in for some tumultuous events as the old deconstructs and is replaced by the new.

Whether our passage through 2012 and beyond is traumatic, filled with fear and panic, or faced with open, trusting hearts connected to higher dimensions of being is up to us. Together we can make it through the Great Shift with a soft landing into a new peaceful, blissful world just waiting to be born. Giving birth, as all women with children know, is painful. How we experience that pain depends on our perception. We can feel it as excruciating or deeply breathe our way through it, knowing it's all worthwhile the moment we hold in our arms the new life we helped create and deeply love.

Life is a Wisdom School

Life is a wisdom school that offers us essential life lessons. The time to learn these lessons, if you have not already done so, is now. Time is accelerating—we'll soon get into why—so learning what you need to the first time a lesson is presented allows you to advance more quickly and to eliminate the increasing drama of failed lessons. Human relationships, for example, offer many opportunities to learn self-acceptance, unconditional love and forgiveness. How long it takes us to master these key lessons is a good indication of where we are in our spiritual development. Wake-up calls are coming louder and more frequently now. So be aware and be prepared.

As you learn and advance, you will gain perspective and understanding that enable you to move wider and higher on the planes of existence, a movement we all will need to master as we navigate the coming transformation to higher forms of consciousness.

A seminary professor taught me something about approaching truth through broadening our perspectives which I've found very useful. He said that in the times in which we're living absolutism is impossible—that is, being sure you know the whole, complete truth. Such dogma reflects limited understanding. My teacher went on to say that relativism was intolerable, as in your truth is yours, mine is mine and both are equally valid. That supports ignorance more than truth. Instead, truth may be approached through perspectivism—the recognition that each of us brings to the table a set of perspectives based on our backgrounds, knowledge, experience and belief systems which are only pieces of a whole we can't see unless we are in conversation with each other. When we communicate in ways that overcome separation, our perspectives become broader and deeper, leading to more understanding of the whole, which is truth. Without this kind of communication and intention to understand, we remain in our narrow constructs and belief systems, which have caused most of the world's wars and divisions.

Arriving at truth is a process, as in the scientific method that starts with a hypothesis, tests it and keeps refining it until the results confirm or deny the hypothesis. Yet, as we now know from the new physics, the observer has an impact on the outcome of an experiment, so truth is never completely objective or separated from our own involvement. We are always learning more, making better connections, and using our own experience as the guide to the answers we seek. Wisdom eventually emerges from this process, and part of wisdom is the humility to recognize our mistakes and to grow from them.

The concept of perspectivism may be illustrated through the universal form of the spiral, where gaining perspective not only takes us wider but higher as well. Just as an eagle flying high can see from her perspective all that's happening in her world, as we develop a broader perspective we begin to see all the pieces as a connected whole of which we are part. That's the most essential learning of all in the wisdom school of Life. We are part of an interconnected web of creation. Mystics across all the great world religions know this. The ancient teachers of wisdom knew this. We are all part of the Creative Universal Intelligence we may call God or Source or Spirit, as is everything in the universe. This consciousness of the wholeness and oneness of what is, has been, and will be is the essence of the Great Shift. If we choose, it will carry us into the higher dimensions of existence where we will gain ever clearer vision as our consciousness moves up and around the spiral toward the Universal Source.

Unity Consciousness is the Way through 2012

Universal or Unity Consciousness, then, is what the Great Shift is about. Those of us who go through the shift and come out the other side on Planet Earth will be part of that consciousness. I want to be one of those, and I trust you do, too. The journey we're going to take together, through this book and through the shift, is going to be the great adventure of our lives. We're blessed to be alive now in human form at the leading edge of what lies ahead. Much depends upon how well we learn our life lessons, gain perspectives, and move along the spiral to higher, Unity Consciousness. This is our work now, as individuals and as the human community of Planet Earth. Our way through 2012 is together, not separately.

Spiritual Wisdom for the Journey

One of our most important lessons as we prepare for 2012 and beyond is not to be afraid of what lies ahead. If your faith tradition draws from the Bible, Torah, or Koran, you know that the angelic realm, the messengers, prefaced their announcements by saying, "Do not be afraid." In order to release our fear, we need to trust that whatever happens will not separate us from our loving Source or from those we love. Each of us plays a part in creating our common future by choosing what we become and what we do. We must not be defeated by forces of darkness, whether within ourselves or coming in through the collective consciousness to which we are connected.

Remember that we are all one, so these forces are part of the "us" that is the entire universe. We can choose not to give power to what divides and harms, instead filling our hearts with love and intentionally connecting to our Source and one another. Love overcomes fear and ignorance because it is a universal connective energy that vibrates at a higher frequency. Think of the vibration of love like the clear musical note the soprano hits that shatters the glass. The high vibration of love creates and expands, while the low vibration of fear and ignorance separates and limits.

Another simple but important lesson is that light, representing higher knowledge, wisdom, and love, illuminates the dark. We must work with and master the range of energies along the spectrum of dark to light. The opening of the gospel of John in the Bible presents us with a deep metaphysical truth: light shines in the darkness and darkness does not overcome it. In an alchemical reaction, light at the vibration of love transmutes the dark into more light. As we shine forth the love and light we are at our essence, we glow in the darkness, overcoming even that which emanates from within us.

Darkness in itself is not harmful or negative. It can precede germination or represent withdrawal from action into contemplation. The night brings rest and dreams needed for the activity of the day. Just as seeds planted in soil germinate and spring into the light, so do human thoughts germinate into intentions and actions. When we speak of dark and light we must not oversimplify by associating one with evil and the other with good. Both are necessary to the whole and are part of the interconnected web of creation. Whenever we encounter what would harm and separate, we offer it love. That's all, and that's enough.

Love is exponentially more powerful in groups, as it brings group energies into resonance at a higher level. That is why we need to learn to work together and form new kinds of communities for the new world we're co-creating with Universal Spirit and with one another. We're going to focus later on how to create intentional, sustainable communities with family, friends, and neighbors as well as around the world and virtually through the internet.

We'll draw on many sources of spiritual wisdom and wisdom traditions in this book. Wisdom is born of spiritual connection, which is its source. More than knowledge, wisdom is using knowledge for its intended purpose, knowing with the heart and the senses, not just the mind. Experience can teach wisdom, but a series of experiences don't necessarily make you wise. It's what you learn from your experience and how it changes you that matters. Learn to recognize wisdom when you encounter it and store it up for when you'll need it. Better yet, become wise yourself.

Nothing is to be hidden from us anymore as we prepare to pass into a higher dimension of knowledge and understanding. That's part of the shift. The world, the heavens and all realms of existence are giving up their secrets to us as we prepare to receive them. Jesus taught that the kingdom of God is within us. I know now what he meant. Through our essential spiritual connection with all that is, all that is is available to us. One of the key phrases attributed to Jesus is "those who have ears to hear, listen." People hear only what they're ready to hear. Jesus spoke in parables or stories which carried different meanings for high initiates in the wisdom schools of the day than for those at the beginning of their spiritual journeys. Masters throughout history told their secrets only to the worthy few who studied for years and passed tests to demonstrate readiness. Now all of that is changing.

Many of us who have studied spiritual wisdom for years are ready to share openly what we have learned. If you can resonate with what I've just said, you are connecting with the kingdom (or kin-dom, as I prefer to call it, where we're all kin) within which you are provided access to all knowledge and to your Source. You have your own direct tie-in to your higher self and through your higher self to any other being at any level of the universe—as you are ready to receive and learn. So as soon as you're ready, you've got a vast set of resources to tap into to learn the wisdom of the past, present, and future—all of which exist at once, at least as potential. Another big lesson we'll get as we move through the shift is that time is not linear but spherical. That's another way of saying that there is no such thing as time, because our consciousness can move around the sphere to any point without going forward or back. The higher dimension Unity Consciousness includes a merging of all time into a natural flow.

After the shift we will not be limited by our belief systems and old paradigm ways of thinking, where power is concentrated in the hands of the few. We will be free, as we always have been, but consciously so, to choose, create, and manifest in no time at all whatever we think or feel. That's why it's so important to raise our own energetic vibrations to that of love, so that our thoughts and feelings will create harmony, peace, and joy. Love raises all boats together. Fear sinks them all separately. We have our work cut out for us. Those who have ears to hear, listen!

PART I: 2012 IS COMING!

CHAPTER ONE: SIGNS OF THE TIMES

In the News

As I sit at my computer, news headlines run across the top of the screen. The latest evidence of the climate change and extreme physical shifts our planet is experiencing pile up: Winter storms and 150 mile per hour winds in California, floods in the Northwest, severe drought and water shortages in the Southeast, record highs or lows in many locations, just in the U.S. alone. Gov. Bill Richardson of New Mexico fires a salvo in what will surely be water wars in our own country, claiming that water-rich states should share with water-limited states, like his own. The eight Great Lakes states and two Canadian provinces respond with a compact to prevent such invasions of their territory. The lakes are already in trouble from a century of pollution and invasive species brought in by foreign vessels.

An intriguing headline grabs my attention: "World's Wacky Weather Getting Weirder." The related article cites rare winter tornadoes in the Midwest, Pacific storms with hurricane-force winds, more than 1000 daily high temperature records and notes this all happened just in the first month of 2008. In addition, twenty of the lower forty-eight states experienced extreme weather events in 2007, the second highest since records have been kept over the last century, according to the National Climatic Data Center in Asheville, NC.

Emails pop up daily from the U.S. Geologic Survey Earthquake Center, reporting earthquake activity around the world. A 5.4 quake along the New Madrid fault in the Midwest takes residents and scientists alike by surprise. The latest conspiracy theory, this one with a 2012 theme, emerges: a highly-placed Norwegian man reports that his government and many others are preparing to save their nations' elite underground when a mysterious planet hits Earth by 2012. Former Vice-President Al Gore accepts the Nobel Peace Prize, calling in his speech upon the United Nations to take leadership now to halt human contributions to global warming before it's too late. Meanwhile, in Bali, the U.S. government, under extreme international pressure, continues to resist efforts to check its massive global pollution.

In Pakistan, opposition leader Benazir Bhutto is assassinated. In Kenya, the newly elected government takes power while thousands riot, protesting the election results. Hundreds are killed. The war in Iraq enters its fifth year, with no end in sight. Signs emerge that the U.S. administration is training its sites on Iran as the next target. Israel once again cuts electricity to the Gaza Strip, leaving the entire Palestinian population without power. Years ago I visited this part of the Middle East and saw first-hand how the oppressed had become the oppressors. Serbia holds an election and an ally of Milosevic is almost elected. In Bosnia I learned the horrors of ethnic cleansing and mass destruction among former Yugoslavian countrymen. Why would power be given back to those who abused it when people have the freedom to choose?

The U.S. Federal Reserve uses its clout and massive reserves to bail out the largest financial institutions in the nation in the midst of an unprecedented credit crisis. Gold shoots through $1000 an ounce, and the dollar falls again against world currencies. China and other countries threaten to turn to the Euro as their currency standard. Housing prices in the U.S. are in free-fall, with the worst yet to come. Michigan, my home state, once the pride of the nation with its thriving auto industry, bears the brunt of the failure of the former Big Three automakers to build energy-efficient vehicles, shedding 400,000 jobs in just seven years. Meanwhile, gas prices soar above $4.00 a gallon, as oil threatens to hit $150 a barrel by year end.

Another article appears in the paper about the faster-than-expected melting of the polar icecaps, and visions of drowning polar bears pop into my head. The Australian government and the environmental organization Green Peace prove heroic by halting parts of the Japanese assault on whales, 950 being their seasonal target, including 50 endangered humpbacks. Species extinction estimates are skyrocketing. I read about expectations of pandemics through bird flu and other animal-to-human virus transfers. Mass migrations are predicted in Africa and elsewhere resulting from drought, famine, and wars. Reports indicate that worldwide food prices have spiked 40% in less than a year. Disaster movies are more frequent on TV: asteroids, floods, and earthquakes along with alien invasions threaten to wipe out the human race, while small teams of brilliant, dedicated scientists work feverishly, using their untested theories to stop the destruction.

Another headline alerts me to a company which designs customized survival plans for individuals, families, agencies, and businesses. They'll send you supplies and even pick you up in an aircraft if you need to be evacuated. It'll only cost you $50,000 up front and $15,000 a year to maintain your preparedness. This is definitely a step up from the old fall-out shelters of my childhood!

The world as we have known it is disappearing rapidly. Did we think we had more time? Do we need more tsunamis and Hurricane Katrinas to convince us that Earth changes in the extreme are underway? Do we still think that governments are going to rescue us in the face of financial collapse on an unprecedented scale? Millions even in the most advanced nations do not have adequate health care. The U.S. alone, with five per cent of the world's population, consumes a quarter of the world's resources. Religious infighting and intolerance are as mean-spirited as ever in the history of the world. Temples and churches close for lack of members. Race, gender, and social class are still issues in the 2008 U.S. presidential election. Malnourished children in underdeveloped nations starve, while malnourished American kids grow obese. The world population has passed 6.6 billion, straining Earth's capacity to sustain life. How many more people can inhabit this planet before we run out of basic resources and kill each other off to stay alive—if disease and disaster don't take us first? Who would want to live in such a world? Is it already here?

Interconnected Systems

I could go on with this litany of evidence that all of the world's systems—physical, geopolitical, economic, technological, health care, educational, and religious—are breaking down or in major transition. You who are paying attention have already noticed this. Your awareness is the first step in expanding your consciousness. Maybe you haven't put it all together yet or realized the enormity of the scale of change underway, but you've surely experienced it first-hand yourself in some way. America's housing foreclosure crisis alone affects everyone who wants to buy or sell a house or even rent a place to live. Everything is related, part of interlocking systems. Nothing is isolated by itself and easy to fix.

A good movie that makes this point is *Mindwalk*. Based on a book by Fritjhof Capra called *The Turning Point*, *Mindwalk* came out in 1990 and stars Sam Waterston as a failed presidential candidate, John Heard as his former publicist-turned-poet who fled to a new life in France, and Liv Ullmann as a brilliant particle physicist who had closed her heart and lost her way. The three of them meet at a sacred site, the tidal island of Mont-Saint-Michel off the Normandy coast of France, and in this mystical setting as the tides flow in and out around them, they engage in a conversation about the nature of the universe and why human endeavors fail. Waterston learns about systems theory and how if one part of a system breaks down or shifts, so will all the systems it is a part of, because everything is connected. As a political leader, he sees that he has to work holistically on systemic change. In the same way, the Great Shift can be impacted positively by those of us who co-create a world without fear and violence. Since we're all part of the system, any one of us can cause a shift in the whole, and a great many of us can make a major impact more rapidly.

Rupert Sheldrake, a biologist who's written many fascinating books, including my favorite, *Dogs Who Know When Their Owners are Coming Home*, years ago introduced the concept of morphogenetic resonance. We're all surrounded by fields of energy, again all interconnected, and as our thoughts and actions energetically interact they cause either resonance, a coherence of vibrating fields, or disharmony, which weakens or lowers the vibrations of the field. Morphic resonance occurs when we all begin to think and act in new ways as we come into resonance with new thoughts. For example, you've probably heard about the hundredth monkey—the one who adopted a new group action of washing her sweet potato before eating it and in so doing completed the critical mass needed to cause a shift in the behavior of all monkeys. Morphic resonance is a higher form of monkey see-monkey do. The influence of the critical mass is enough to impact the whole into a higher consciousness, a form of evolution by transformation.

In the same way, some estimate if 1% of the world population, now totaling over 6.6 billion, were to become enlightened, that is, resonant with the higher vibration dimension we are moving into, they would constitute the critical mass needed to shift the consciousness of the whole planet. That's what their spiritual guidance tells them. If that's so, then the more people who are aware of and choose this path, the more likely we are to experience a soft landing in the coming Great Shift rather than mass trauma. The higher the vibration we collectively hold, the more people will entrain or become resonant with it and shift into the Unity Consciousness. We can also entrain downward if we go into fear, so we need to hold the higher intention at all times.

We're all going to have to make some very important choices in the very near future. Do we live in the same way we have, consuming more than our fair share of the world's resources, assuming an unlimited supply, ignoring the poverty and disparities in life style between the have-and have-not communities and nations? Do we continue to over harvest our seas and pollute our waterways with toxic chemicals which then enter our bodies, leading to more cancer, disease, and drugs? Do wars continue or finally end? Will humanity find a way through to a bright future or perish as Earth cleanses herself of a species she'd be better off without?

In the mid-nineties I experienced a powerful example of systems theory at a conference, "The Spirit of Place", held by the Whidbey Institute for Earth, Spirit, and Community on Whidbey Island, WA. The Whidbey Institute (www.whidbeyinstitute.org) provides models you may want to explore for creating intentional community and sustainable ecology. The Institute also trains new leadership for the kind of world thoughtful human endeavor can create.

"The Spirit of Place" illustrated how powerfully people are attached to the place they call "home." Each of the participants was asked to bring a picture of what felt like home, even if he or she no longer lived there. One woman brought a picture of a swing in her grandmother's yard, a place she loved when growing up. I brought a picture of the ranch we used to have in New Mexico, a mystical, magical land which still captures my heart. A local ecologist spent several days teaching us about the nature of ecosystems. Each has similar features but is different in form and type of habitat. Each healthy region provides habitat for all its species, along with corridors allowing wildlife to move from one ecosystem to another, if their habitat is endangered by human activity or Earth changes. Many people complain about deer eating their gardens, yet fail to recognize that their developments have displaced the deer population's natural habitat. One development I used to live in wanted to kill off the local beaver population because it had dammed up a small tributary of a creek near someone's house! Near my current home a local beaver population lives in our pond, and we are adapting to them as they are adapting to us. We must learn to respect all species, because ecosystems can survive without humans but not without other forms of life. We are the expendable ones in the food chain!

Watersheds are the backbone of a region's ecosystem, as water enters, flows through and out of the system, bringing nourishment to all species within. If waterways are diverted or go dry, the implications for life in the ecosystem are critical. Another favorite old movie of mine, *The Milagro Beanfield War*, set in rural northern New Mexico, tells the tale of a power struggle between the local Hispanic landowners and greedy developers who wanted to divert the ecosystem's water for a wealthy golf community—in the midst of the high desert! The actions of one outraged, creative man, supported by his local community, foiled the plans of the developers, and harmony was restored to the land.

On a much larger scale, the threats of water diversion from the Great Lakes Basin ecosystem, which holds nearly 20% of the world's fresh water, are growing more serious, as water-poor states think piping or trucking in Great Lakes water will solve their problems of drought and over-development. Such short-sighted destruction of one of the main ecosystems of the planet would have disastrous consequences.

Do you know about your local and regional watersheds? Do you know what species besides the human depend on them for life? Most of us haven't a clue. Yet some in my area of North Carolina are now better informed as a result of an extreme drought we've experienced, possibly the worst in at least 800 years! Despite the need for water conservation, local municipalities were exceedingly slow to respond to the severity of the problem. Living where we do, water shortages were a new thing for most of them. My husband and I left New Mexico when we foresaw that water wars were a likely part of that state's future, and now we were hearing about them in an area we thought was water-rich. A recent newspaper article described in detail the watershed we depend on here, the first I'd seen about it since arriving over five years ago.

Knowledge of your local ecosystem is an essential part of your preparation for the coming Earth changes. Do you live in an area prone to floods, drought, earthquakes, volcanoes, hurricanes or tornadoes? Expect uncommonly extreme patterns in the coming years. Learn what could happen in your area and get a copy of your municipality's emergency preparedness plan. You may want to critique it for them if you think it's inadequate. For example, we learned from Hurricane Katrina in 2005 that emergency evacuation plans didn't include people's companion or domestic animals. Some people refused to leave without them. Enormous animal and human suffering that was preventable resulted from a lack of adequate preparations on the parts of individuals and government agencies.

I say these things not to create fear but to encourage people to face the possibilities of what lies ahead. A former Girl Scout, I haven't forgotten the Scout motto: "Be Prepared." If you're aware and prepared, you can handle situations, even the unexpected, with a minimum of fear and disruption. It's the element of surprise that results in panic and chaos. Being prepared is essential, regardless of whether or not the need to enact our emergency plans ever arrives. We'll cover how to do that in Part II: Preparing for the Great Shift.

Signs of Hope

While being prepared does involve anticipating the worst, we certainly don't want to expect the worst will happen. We prepare for it, then let it go and focus our attention on a better outcome. In the next chapter we'll look at five possible scenarios on the path to 2012 and beyond, some more hopeful than others. In anticipation of that, let's take a look at the more positive signs of the times.

One hopeful sign is that people are connecting with each other and creating new communities more than ever before in human history, courtesy of the internet. Virtual social networks, like www.MySpace.com, www.YouTube.com, and www.Facebook.com, provide opportunities for people to build communication skills and creativity. That's not to say that all that's out there on the web is positive. The same avenues of communication can be used to criticize people and institutions, to promote fanaticism, conspiracy, and pleasure-seeking rather than true community—people connecting heart-to-heart and offering support for each other and creative options for the whole community. We'll talk more about building intentional and sustainable community in Chapter Six. For now, before the Great Shift, we get to practice our communications and community-building skills on the internet—at least as long as mass communications systems work, something we're expecting could be disrupted more and more as we pass through a period of intense solar flares and electromagnetic disruptions peaking around 2011-2012. Part of a good preparation plan includes methods of staying in touch with your basic communities in the event of communications breakdowns that last several days or longer. Hint: computers and cells phones won't work!

The internet is also a great tool for the fast exchange of information—not necessarily knowledge and usually not wisdom—but information. Nobody makes a living as an encyclopedia salesperson these days. Instead, there are search engines and Wikipedia. Sorting through what's important and useful is always a challenge, but access to virtually (pun intended) any information is coming, if not already here. And because of the immediacy and ease with which information may be exchanged, what I said earlier about things not being able to be hidden for long is more in evidence. Personal web sites can be thrown up in a matter of minutes on social networks. Many people have learned that they don't want so much personal information posted for all the world to see. Some invent new personas and seek love in all the wrong places. The internet is value-neutral. It is you who must exercise your own values in its use. Plagiarism among students is both more widespread and more often caught because of the internet than ever before. Professors have access to the same sources students do.

One sign of our changing times is Queen Elizabeth's posting her official Christmas, 2007 message on YouTube to reach the widest possible audience! I remember watching her coronation on a seven-inch green and white TV screen fifty-five years ago. We've come a long way in global communications. The internet enables us to have networks all over the world. It's fast, cheap, and universally available. When third-world kids get wind-up laptops that hook them up to the wireless internet, improved universal educational access will bring us closer to world peace.

Children are our hope for the future in more ways than we usually mean when we say that. The children coming into the world now and who have come as early as forty years ago, often called Indigos, Crystals, and Rainbows (detailed in Chapter Eight), bring with them new, higher vibrations and advanced intuition and empathic skills. They communicate through their senses and psychically in ways that haven't been seen on Earth before. Watch the movies *The Last Mimzy* and *The Golden Compass* for a look at the powers and love of these children. It is they who will lead us into the future.

The most hopeful sign of all is that people are waking up spiritually and choosing the path of transformation—personal, political, and global. We are yearning for a peaceful world with enough for all. As we reconnect with our Source, the God of our hearts and understanding, no matter what our faith traditions or belief systems, we will no longer see ourselves, our ethnic groups, religions, and nations as separate—distinct, perhaps, but not separate. Instead, we will recognize the essential oneness of all that is and will call for an equal playing field for all people to fulfill their potential, not only out of spiritual recognition of our oneness but also out of necessity. The gifts and talents of each person and the resources of the entire planet must be used only for what is for the highest good of each and every one of us, for all of life and all that sustains life, especially for Mother Earth herself.

The New Spirituality

The new spirituality represented by Unity Consciousness is transcending old paradigm hierarchical, male-dominated, dogma- and doctrine-based religious structures. People are finding the kingdom of God within themselves. Just as the Protestant Reformation of old focused on the personal relationship between the self and God, rejecting the need for a priest as intermediary, so too people today are finding their own spiritual guidance through direct communication with and experience of the Divine, however they define that. They are forming their own spiritual networks for guidance and support. The time for gurus and their devoted followers is past. Direct access to spiritual knowledge and wisdom is readily available, and one needn't be a part of a traditional faith community to participate.

Many continue to belong to their churches and temples because they find support and guidance there, and as long as these communities continue to serve the needs of their members they will survive. Yet the demographics speak for themselves. The long, slow decline of mainstream religious structures is much in evidence. Those that are growing tend to be more conservative in nature, offering their members a ready-made set of beliefs and behaviors that discourage independent thought and action. That is old paradigm and will not endure. The denomination in which I served as an ordained minister has declined precipitously in membership, giving, and spiritual leadership during more than twenty years of debating whether gays and lesbians may serve in church leadership. No matter which side of the argument they were on, church members left in droves, in many cases electing not to join other congregations but to encounter God on their own terms.

We still need good spiritual teachers to help people along their paths, those who recognize that they haven't all the answers but rather a measure of wisdom gained through knowledge and experience to share, along with a desire to encourage people to find their own paths and realize fully their own spiritual being and life lessons. This kind of leadership is more like mentoring than the traditionally priestly role of the one chosen by God as intermediary for the whole community. It is inclusive and empowering, a more feminine style of leadership, symbolized by the circle of wholeness. The masculine symbol is the pyramid, with male authority at the top and the masses on the bottom.

Recovering the Divine Feminine

In our own time both male and female energies must be brought into balance and harmony. A deep infusion of the feminine divine is called for to balance the aggressive male energy which has dominated and disempowered much of the world. Dan Brown's wildly popular novel *The DaVinci Code*, published in 2003, touched a deep chord in the human spirit and made a huge contribution to the story and the energy of the divine feminine in history and the human heart. Concerning the critical mass mentioned earlier that can shift the consciousness of the whole, I figure that one percent or more of the world's population either read the book, saw the movie version or heard Brown's story of the restoration of Mary Magdalene to her rightful place as Jesus' bride and the mother of his child, herself the holy grail, receiving the blood of Christ and enabling his bloodline to continue down to the present age. Resonating with tens of millions, this version of history (or should we say herstory?) has opened minds and hearts, contributing to the Great Shift.

On a metaphysical level—more important than the literal— the story is about feminine kundalini, the creative energy which arises from deep within, merging through the transforming power of love with masculine kundalini to produce a new higher order, spiritually evolved kind of being—pure, whole, filled with love and light. This new being is the very image of the Divine, reflecting the Creator's intention for the Unity or Christ Consciousness born of this union to enter the world and allow the old, limited, lower consciousness to dissolve.

As the Unity Consciousness is grounded on the planet, life on Earth and throughout the cosmos is renewed. Rain falls, rivers flow, crops grow, animals and humans give birth—the cycles of creation continue undisturbed. But take away the power of the Divine Mother, as has happened in the past 10,000 years, and the world becomes a violent expression of a domineering male principle. Wholeness and balance can only be restored when she is acknowledged and empowered as Queen and creates with her King new life that re-enchants the world. It has always been a part of our mythology and collective consciousness. Now the energy of the new consciousness allows us a foretaste of the glorious experience that we have to look forward to as we conclude the Great Shift, a restoration of wholeness and well-being on the planet we call home, a new beginning for humanity and for Earth as well.

The New Synthesis of Science and Spirit

Just as the Unity Consciousness marries masculine and feminine principles and energies, so does the newly emerging synthesis of science and spirit. The male linear, logical kind of thinking and creativity is blended with the feminine intuitive, sensory kind of feeling and creativity to open new horizons and levels of understanding and experience for humanity. The most significant challenge for humanity at present is coming to recognize the interconnectedness of all life and all which sustains life. Knowing that through experience of spiritual connection, not just believing in it, will mean an end to the old paradigm of separation and the suffering it causes. While systems theory in the sciences offers useful perspectives, it is through one's own mystical experience at a deeply spiritual level that everything in the universe is one interconnected whole that the concept becomes real.

From the smallest particle to the largest mass, from a simple idea to a complex organization, from the dim past to the distant future, from our three-dimensional world to a multidimensional, holographic universe where death is only the moment of transition to another way of being—everything is continually drawn into relationship through a conscious, universal field of intention and its urge to unite all that is. What appears to separate from one part of the field reappears in another.

Watch cells grow under a microscope. Follow the ripples of a stone thrown into a stream. Observe how someone you're thinking of contacts you. A vast field of energy commanded by the Creative Spirit of Love lies all around and within us. I have experienced this field and know that it exists. As we intentionally align with this Unified Field of Love and allow its high vibration energy to flow and express its love through us, we participate in creating greater wellbeing and wholeness for the entire field. We influence the field, and the field influences us.

The leading edge of humanity has evolved in its consciousness to knowing that the impulse toward union and the harmony and balance it brings is greater than that of separation and dissonance. Recognizing that we are part of a much greater whole does not diminish any of us but rather multiplies all that we are and expands all that we create.

An understanding of quantum physics will end the paradigm of hierarchical, male dominance of a mechanistic universe of separate parts. Energy is everything, and everything is energy. Matter—focused energy—can exist in more than one place at a time. As the observer interacts with the observed, particles of energy move and the field shifts. A good film that illustrates and explains this quantum world we inhabit, *What the Bleep Do We*

Know!?, appeared in 2004. Its much expanded later version, *What the Bleep!?—Down the Rabbit Hole*, includes interviews with a wide array of scientists and spiritual teachers who illuminate each others' perspectives. I highly recommend it. As we said earlier, combining perspectives broadens our understanding of the whole but is still limited by what we don't know and haven't yet experienced. Here in the quantum universe the realms of Science and Spirit meet. The physicist becomes the mystic. The mystic smiles.

It is now humanity's task to build bridges from the old consciousness of domination, dualism, and separation in a mechanistic universe to a new consciousness of Unity, the interconnected web of life that resides within and around each of us and celebrates the creative expression of love in all its myriad forms. Our new work is to collaborate and co-create with the Unified Field of Love all that we are capable of being through the high vibration of the Field. Humankind is now free to reach not only the stars but also the height, breadth, and depth of human potential, joy, and creativity. As we merge into the Unity Consciousness, our understanding and our hearts give birth to something new. While we have much to experience before the Great Shift is complete, we trust and know that it will be for the highest good of all.

Home for all of us is Earth, Mother Earth, the living being whose consciousness we call Gaia. She has nurtured and nourished us and all her inhabitants for eons. Now she is feeling the effects of cycles of change and the human-caused pollution and toxic energy that need to be released so that she can be healthy once again. As a friend of mine said, Gaia is uncomfortable and needs to shake her hips and move around a bit to get more comfortable. Releasing pressure and toxins may cause significant damage on Earth's surface. Add to this increased solar flare activity, expected to peak in 2011-2012, which leads to satellite and communications breakdowns and you have the potential for mass chaos and panic—unless you're able to stay in your heart center, the point of your connection to the universe. Breathe deeply, release any anxiety, trust that all happens for a purpose and know that you are an eternal spirit connected to the One Spirit. Ultimately we will all need to surrender to this knowledge, gained through our experience with Spirit, to make it through the shift in physical form. And if we don't, that's all right, too. It really is. You'll still be you—just not necessarily in your current physical body. Your loved ones will still be connected to you through the vibration of love. They always will. Trust and surrender. Stay in the heart. All shall be well.

The signs of the times, then, point not toward neat, orderly evolution but rather to messy, chaotic transformation. The new science teaches us that systemic breakdowns and chaos always precede the emergence of new, self-organizing forms. Life forms no longer viable die out and re-emerge as something not quite the same, something new. Death followed by new life is an old story, as old as life itself. What we are observing now and living through is the end of life as we know it and the beginning of a profoundly changed world. The nature of that world is yet to be known.

CHAPTER TWO: A GUIDE TO 2012
PREDICTIONS AND POSSIBILITIES

Many believe that 2012 marks the anticipated date of the Great Shift to Unity Consciousness. Despite a growing and often confusing body of literature, lore, and websites focusing on the significance of 2012, the common expectation is that something big is coming. Exactly what and when remain to be seen. Given the uncertainty, it's important to develop and use your own process of discernment to guide your path through the years leading to and through 2012.

Spiritual Guidance and Discernment

You have within you your connection with higher guidance. You may call that guidance God, Spirit, Guides, Angels, Source, your Higher Self, or something else. Whether you are aware of them or not, many Beings of Light or spirits in dimensions other than the one we see and experience in our three-dimensional world can offer us knowledge and wisdom. These beings are not in physical form but exist as energy signatures of light that some people can see or communicate with. There are also those forces, here in 3D or in other dimensions, which will try to deflect us off our path to Unity Consciousness for their own reasons and purposes. Religious, spiritual, science fiction, and fantasy literature are full of examples of these beings in other realms. As people become more open to communicating with Beings of Light and as the veils between dimensions thin, these encounters will become more common. Many people already sense on occasion the presence of loved ones who have transitioned through death, and that is one common form such encounters take.

In order to stay centered in light from the highest spiritual realms at the energetic vibration of love, you may call at any time upon God or whatever Beings of Lights in the higher dimensions you feel connected to for guidance and clarity about anything that confuses you in your life. Sometimes answers come to you in prayer or meditation, through other people, even in synchronicities— someone will phone or show up at just the right time or you're delayed unaccountably and as a result something good happens or you miss being in an accident. You know the kind of thing I mean. Unity Consciousness brings with it highly developed intuition and heightened senses and perception. It expands your creativity and capacity to manifest or bring about whatever you are thinking or desiring. Trust that you have access within you to the higher realms for guidance in making informed, wise, and loving choices.

The choices we make in 3D are generally based on either analytical processes (the head) or dominant emotions (the heart). In the higher consciousness, the head and the heart will work together, with the heart taking the lead. We will choose not just what is best for ourselves but the most loving outcome for all concerned. This insight came to me as I was reflecting on a dynamic I'd observed when imbalances of power are present between people in relationships. I would describe it as a dominant force pushing against a weaker object until it meets resistance. Resistance then strengthens the weaker side until it reaches equilibrium with the stronger force, and the situation is resolved through balance. The attempt to dominate on the one hand and to resist domination on the other is a dynamic, whether enacted between couples, co-workers, or nations, with far-reaching consequences for the world we live in. The Cold War operated on such a dynamic. It promotes separation over unity, competition over cooperation, war over peace.

It's time we humans learned another way, one which sages, avatars, and peacemakers have advocated throughout time: discerning and choosing the most loving outcome. That may not necessarily be the easiest, quickest, or most expedient response, but it is the most effective and personally satisfying. It's also the answer to the question asked by the movement in the '90's, "What Would Jesus Do?", and it doesn't matter whether you claim to be a follower of Jesus, Buddha, Krishna or other spiritual master, it's always the best choice. The most loving thing is that which aligns you with love, the most powerful force in the universe. How to choose the most loving thing in any situation and accept the consequences of that choice are a part of the challenge each of us faces as we move toward the Great Shift. You will need to attune to your guidance and ask for what is the most loving thing you can offer, say, or do, as occasions present themselves. Is it backing off from a fight, is it speaking the truth as you see it with love, is it joining with others to bring about needed change? As you discover what may be approaching on the way to 2012, hold in your consciousness the concept of the most loving thing as a standard to help bring about the Unity Consciousness and the softest possible landing into 2012 and beyond.

Prophecies, Predictions, Possibilities and Probabilities

To explain the significance of 2012, we'll turn to the many prophecies, predictions, probabilities and possibilities that have been floating around, some for thousands of years, some rather recent. Regardless of where they come from and how long they've been around, all of these converge on the period around 2011 to 2013, and most specifically focus on the rapidly approaching date of the winter solstice, December 21, 2012.

The most important and most extensive of the prophecies has to do with the Mayan calendar. Many books have been written on the subject, which I suggest you delve into if you're drawn to them. My favorites are Carl Calleman's *The Mayan Calendar and the Transformation of Consciousness* and Barbara Hand Clow's *The Mayan Code*. These and other 2012 resources are listed in Appendix B.

The Maya were an ancient, advanced civilization—at least until dark forces led them into a downward spiral with war, bloodshed, and human sacrifice. When we speak of the Maya in connection with 2012, we're talking about a culture whose amazing city-states, spread across the Yucatan peninsula of Mexico into Guatemala, Honduras, and Belize, were independent but connected through trade and communication. The Mayan knowledge of the cosmos, evident in the alignments of their pyramids and temples, was as advanced as the Egyptian. Mayan shamans kept an astonishingly accurate cosmic calendar of immense importance still relevant today. This calendar gives us the most information about why 2012 is significant and what is likely to occur then. In a nutshell, on the winter solstice, December 21, 2012, many significant cycles of the Mayan calendar come to an end before beginning all over again. It is the end of the great cycle of the Precession of the Equinoxes, a 25,950 year cycle during which Earth, wobbling on its axis, completes a revolution around the solar system and begins a new cycle. 2012 also marks Earth's movement out of the astrological sign of Pisces, where it has been since the time of Jesus, a period of around 2160 years, into the Age of Aquarius.

Remember the movie from the '60's, *Hair* ? The title song spoke of the dawning of this Age of Aquarius. The psychedelic generation of the hippies got there first with LSD, but now none of that is needed for us to access the cosmic forces which are leading us into the Aquarian Age, envisioned as a Golden Age of peace, harmony, creativity, and love, the fulfillment of human potential.

If we humans as a species make it into the Unity Consciousness before we do ourselves in or before the Earth rids herself of us, we will have evolved into an awareness that we are multidimensional beings in a multidimensional universe. While some 2012 interpreters say that we'll move from the third dimension material world into the fifth dimension, there's no common agreement on that, and I don't think it matters what we call the next dimension we enter, as long as we recognize that it's much expanded beyond 3D.

The earlier image I presented of the spiraling evolution of consciousness, wider and higher, is all about that. The higher we raise our vibration or frequency, the more we will resonate with the higher and wider realms of existence and leave behind our limited visions and derisions. We literally create heaven on Earth. Jesus' prayer asked that God's will be done on Earth as it is in the realm called Heaven. Like many sayings attributed to Jesus, this one is packed with levels of meaning. "As above, so below" is the expression of a basic cosmic natural law, that Earth is a reflection, a microcosm, of the heavens. Bringing Heaven to Earth, manifesting it here in all its glory and splendor, has been the task, the goal of the ancient, advanced civilizations and the mystics of all times. They understood the cosmos in ways that we have lost but are rapidly recovering as we get in touch with and unlock ancient mysteries like the Mayan calendar.

The cosmic calendar of the Maya, which is kept with precise accuracy even today, reveals cycles in the evolution of human consciousness. Calleman's book substantiates this with great insight and brilliance. A Swedish scientist enlightened by his own spiritual search, Calleman has linked himself with the Oneness Movement begun in India by a sage named Bhagavan and his wife Amma. This movement trains people who come to Bhagavan's community in India to offer what is called Deeksha (or Diksha), an energetic transmission at a very high vibration through the crowns of recipients who are seeking enlightenment or illumination at a spiritual, mental, emotional, and physical level. I have received Deeksha a number of times and have found it to be an aid, along with other forms of spiritual energy healing (which I offer and teach), to releasing what no longer serves us and bringing us into harmony and balance. Calleman has advocated combining worldwide meditation, another form of giving and receiving Deeksha, at specific dates significant in the Mayan calendar in order to bring the needed critical mass, 1% or more of the population, to Unity Consciousness more quickly, in time for the Great Shift of 2012.

For on that winter solstice, our planet Earth will be aligned with the Sun and the dark rift of the Galactic Center of the Milky Way, at which time some believe a huge energetic burst of light will lift us into a higher dimension, an energetic frequency for which we, hopefully, will be ready. In that higher, wider dimension we will have direct access to the knowledge and wisdom of the universe and take our place in the cosmos as a fully evolved humanity, moving beyond violence and war, fear and distrust.

Those who study the Mayan calendar have much more to say about the details of the transformation of consciousness already underway and expected to culminate in 2012. The calendar shows a series of cycles within a total of nine "underworlds" or epochs going back to the "Big Bang" over 15 billion years ago. The calendar's Great Cycle or Long Count, when the Maya in all likelihood began to keep time, started over five thousand years ago in 3114 B.C.E. The Mayan priests and elders selected as Timekeepers calculated the precise completion of the Precession of the Equinoxes. Each underworld contains cycles of seven days and six nights, like the first creation story in Genesis, covering periods of time. As each cycle completes and the next one begins, it accelerates twenty times. The seventh underworld lasted 256 years, while the eighth, which we are in right now, takes only 12.8 years. In 2008 as I write, we are in the Fifth Night of the Eighth (Galactic) Underworld, which is characterized by the collapse of lower consciousness institutions, just as we have been experiencing. In previous similar periods, we saw the fall of the Roman Empire, the Great Depression, and World War II. The ninth and final underworld, the Universal, begins in 2011/2012 and completes in only 260 days, twenty times faster than the preceding cycle.

As the end of the Mayan Calendar approaches, we have a sense of time either standing still or moving at blazing speed, until time is no more. That is one way we will know we are closer to the Great Shift. Linear time loses its grip on us, and us on it. Time becomes spherical—past, present, and future merge and may be experienced from any point on the sphere. We see things from that high, wide spiral of the eagle in flight rather from the three dimensional Earth plane and can travel from one point to another without going backwards or forwards.

In addition to the Great Cycle, the Precession of the Equinoxes, other lesser cycles or octaves of the Mayan calendar complete on December 21, 2012. The conjunction of all of these cycles, most occurring over thousands of years, makes this date so significant. An event of cosmic proportions has been predicted for at least five thousand years.

While Calleman and others have recalculated the calendar and believe that it actually completes on October 28, 2011, and another group has seen Feb. 13, 2013 as the completion date, the weight of prophecy points to Winter Solstice, 2012. As we experience time as one fluid stream, we needn't lock ourselves into one specific date when the Great Shift will take place, but rather a set of conditions that will occur, are occurring and have already occurred. To the extent that we can perceive them and go into and with the flow of them, we will pass through an opening in Earth's energetic grid into a new way of being.

The Maya appear to have believed that some kind of cataclysm would occur at the completion of the Long Count. We do know that the lineup of Earth, Sun, and Galactic Center can have tremendous power, but we don't know exactly what to expect. Not long ago a group I was with in Mexico was privileged to participate in a sacred ceremony with two Mayan elder-shamans at an ancient temple hidden within Palenque, a major Mayan city-state. They were keepers of what they claimed was one of four authentic ancient Mayan crystal skulls (another Mayan elder speaks of 52, with about half yet to be found), which contained a spirit of prophecy. I asked the younger shaman what he expected would happen in 2012. His response: "Nothing. The Maya are back." His enigmatic reply seemed to indicate that the higher consciousness of his ancestors was once again anchored in the ancient places of power and in the minds and hearts of his people. So may it be. As we await the end of the Mayan calendar's prophecy, let's turn to other prophecies and predictions to see if they will help us discern what is likely to happen.

Hopi Prophecy

Staying with prophecies of native peoples, the Hopi have had a prediction about the end of the Fourth World and the beginning of the Fifth for hundreds of years. Without going into all the details, it involves a series of nine signs which when complete signal the end of the world as we know it and the emergence of a new world. According to a Hopi elder quoted on the internet, the ninth sign is as follows: "You will hear of a dwelling-place in the heavens, above the earth, that will fall with a great crash. It shall appear as a blue star. Very soon after this, the ceremonies of my people will cease. ...These are the signs that great destruction is coming...." The prophecy goes on to describe this destruction, which sounds like nuclear war and its devastation. It says that those who understand the prophecy and stay in the sacred places of the Hopi people will survive. Following this catastrophe, Pahana, the lost white brother, will return and the Fifth World will dawn. The reference to Pahana is a common element in many prophecies, including the Christian, in which a savior figure returns and ushers in a new golden age.

The apocalyptic account of the ninth sign is also echoed in other Doomsday prophecies.

Interestingly, in October, 2007, a periodic comet known as P17/Holmes appeared and brightened nearly a million times overnight. The field around it appeared blue and at one point was larger than the sun. This phenomenon has been interpreted by some as evidence of the ninth sign, the blue star, sometimes referred to as the blue sun. Those who follow the blue sun, according to the prophecy, will survive, while those who follow the red sun will perish. The blue sun followers will be the more spiritually awakened. Those who resist the Great Shift will perish. Has the ninth sign been fulfilled? Many believe that it has. But the Hopi have the final word. Watch to see how they are interpreting this phenomenon.

Ojibway Prophecy

Another ancient prophecy, dating from the ninth century, comes from the Ojibway people. According to one of seven prophecies in their tradition, in the time of the Seventh Fire (the current age) people will be given a choice to walk a path leading to healing of the Earth and its inhabitants or to take the path of destruction. If they chose the healing path, an Eighth Fire will be lit and usher in eternal peace. As with similar prophecies, it is up to the individual in concert with his or her spiritual guidance to discern the meaning of the message.

Channeled Messages

Many spiritually awakened people have developed the capacity to bring through messages from higher dimensional sources. While this may challenge your sense of reality, western religious traditions recognize saints and angels, while eastern traditions recognize, among others, ascended masters, or highly evolved beings who completed their passages through human form and now exist in a higher plane from which they guide those on earth. Jesus, Buddha, Krishna, Mother Mary, Sai Baba, St. Germaine, Thoth, Kuthumi, Djwahl Kuhl and others are among the most well known of these. The Archangels Michael, Raphael, and Gabriel appear in biblical sources, and their messages are also accessible today.

There are many other Archangels and orders of angels available to us. Millions of people call upon these and other Beings of Light who exist in higher dimensions as energetic presences for guidance and support. A great many of us now are able to act as conduits for these beings to bring through their guidance and messages for us because we are able to hold a high enough vibration or frequency to allow us to connect with them. This is not only because of our intention but also because the higher realms have worked with us over time to create and prepare the channels or conduits through which communications may take place.

Channeling is simply bringing through our own conscious-ness one or a group of higher consciousness entities for the benefit of an individual or group. This capacity can be activated in anyone. It is different from mediumship, which people like John Edward, James Van Praagh, or Alison DuBois practice when they work with entities in what we call the astral plane, where beings no longer in human form exist but not necessarily in a higher dimension. They and we who channel may also access the Akashic Records, or the energy field of the collective consciousness that contains all thought, emotion, and experiences of humanity throughout time.

Some individuals are known for long-term relationships with beings in other dimensions or star systems, such as Tom Kenyon with the Hathors, Barbara Hand Clow and Barbara Marciniak with the Pleiadians, the Rev. Terri Newlon with Ascended Master Djwhal Khul, the Rev. Maia Nartoomid with Ascended Master Thoth, and several people with Ascended Master Kuthumi. All have websites, listed in Appendix B, and most have archived messages you can access. Numerous people connect frequently with other masters, saints, and angels. Jesus is available to all who call on him at any time, as are Mother Mary and Mary Magdalene—representing the Divine Masculine and Divine Feminine energies. Most religions teach their adherents to call upon higher beings or essences for clarity and support. Given that, it is not much of a leap to expand the field of assistance you may call upon and connect with.

For those of you for whom this is new or unbelievable, I suggest that you keep an open mind and heart. The spirits of all of us continue after death, or shedding the human form, and continue to exist. We are eternal in our connection with Source energy. Is it so far-fetched that advanced beings would make themselves available to us for guidance, love, and support? Have you ever felt the presence of a loved one who has crossed through death? I often experience the energy and presence of the loved ones of people I work with in spiritual energy healing. The vibration of the energy work gives them a connection so that they can come through for a brief period and convey through thought or presence their love for the person to whom they're connected. It happens all the time. Maybe now that you're aware of that, you'll recognize these connections when they happen and even ask for them. I suggest speaking to your loved ones who've crossed over and asking for or offering forgiveness and expressing love and gratitude. Just as you may pray to God, Jesus, or another non-visible being and connect with that energy, so may you connect to others who exist in other planes. I personally call upon Beings of Light in higher realms regularly for clarity, guidance, and support. You have only to ask. And because you have free will, you need to ask. Most will not connect without an invitation. If you do attract lower vibration energies, tell them firmly to leave or go to the highest light.

That was all by way of introduction to the channeled messages which a number of people have been receiving in recent months and years. I subscribe to the email newsletters of a number of people whose channeled information is consistently of a high quality and resonance. Part of your own discernment process is to see whether you resonate with the messages that come through. Are they credible? Do they connect with your own intuition, your own sense of the possible? Group discernment is also helpful, and I regularly consult with others whose judgment, intuition, and experience I trust to make sure I'm getting messages clearly. After all, we each have our own filters or perspectives through which we sense and feel what is "true," although we have only partial glimpses of that. As the apostle Paul said in his letter to the Corinthian church, "Now we see but a poor reflection as in a mirror; then we shall see face to face" (First Corinthians 13:12, New International Version).

The Hathors, a group consciousness of interdimensional, intergalactic beings channeled by Tom Kenyon, occasionally send significant messages that Tom posts on his website, www. tomkenyon.com, and emails around. Their message of November 14, 2007 was dire. It warned of a "perilous passage" through 2008. They speak of more frequent and serious Earth changes, geopolitical shifts, and planetary challenges from within and without. We are encouraged to continue our pathways to personal transformation, preparing ourselves for the coming shift, and they suggest that we create through our intention and visualization a holon, or protective geometric light form consisting of an upward pointing and a downward pointing tetrahedron (four-sided pyramid), around ourselves whenever things get rough. I was personally surprised to hear them say that until the summer of 2007 it was not certain that humans would survive the changes that would take place on Planet Earth. In March, 2008, the Hathors spoke of a morphing of the Earth's magnetic field arising from energies in deep space that will continue for several years. They recommended attuning to the Earth's core and the Galactic core to create more stability within our own magnetic energy fields.

Master Kuthumi, known as the World Teacher, has spoken to me and others of various changes that may occur between now and 2012. It is he and the rest of the Spiritual Hierarchy of Ascended

Masters, also known by the ancient name of the Great White Brotherhood, who encouraged me to write this book. He confirms that significant Earth changes will take place and that life as we know it will not continue. We are not to fear, as these changes are necessary in order for Earth to be prepared for the coming Great Shift to higher consciousness. There is more, but suffice it to say that we are getting information and guidance from many sources which confirm that something big is coming in these years leading up to and beyond 2012.

Doomsday Predictions

What list would be complete without the Doomsday predictions which have been around forever? They are part of the collective consciousness, whether from what has happened in the past or what may happen in the future. These include Armageddon, the Rapture, and Judgment Day—interpretations from biblical sources— but may also be found in other religious traditions. The focus is typically on a catastrophic event—a battle or act of God—which results in the death of all but a faithful remnant—144,000 is a number commonly heard—who survive and/or are taken up into a higher dimension. Actually, some parts of this relate to the 2012 predictions, but the key difference is that the process of Earth's and her inhabitants' ascension into a higher dimension of consciousness is not based on God's wrath or judgment but rather God's love. Based in love, not fear, the Great Shift is seen as necessary to preserve life on Earth as well as to allow all beings to find a place in the universe that has been prepared for them, one of the many mansions of God's house Jesus talked about.

Now that we've covered the main prophecies and predictions, let's be more specific about the kinds of changes that might occur. In Part II we'll look at how to prepare ourselves for them.

Earth periodically undergoes cycles of change. Some of the natural phenomena that have happened before and could happen again are another ice age (the last ice age ended about 10,000 years ago), tectonic plate shifts causing earthquakes, volcanic eruptions, solar flare activity, climate change, extensive wild fires, hurricanes, cyclones and tornadoes, asteroids or comets hitting earth, and even a pole shift caused by weakening electromagnetic fields and gravitational pull. Each of these phenomena—and there are more—could cause changes we would consider catastrophic, even though they may be natural. Changing temperatures of land and sea can cause massive species extinction, prolonged drought or floods, famine, and mass migration, among other things. Some of these could happen rapidly, others over longer periods of time.

In addition, the possibility of pandemics caused by bird flu, West Nile virus or other bacterial or viral sources could wipe out millions. Diseases like HIV-AIDS and E-coli have already devastated whole populations, especially in the under-developed nations of Africa. The flu and polio epidemics, part of my parents' experience, could resurface in even more virulent forms. Species mutations leading to new diseases are highly possible.

One has only to read science fiction or watch the Sci Fi Channel to discover the whole range of possible disasters connected with Earth changes and their consequences. My father, an engineer, was an avid science fiction reader, and I was exposed to the range of possibilities at an early age. I even taught a university course in classic science fiction years ago. All of the worst case scenarios are out there in the popular imagination.

But you don't need to be a sci fi aficionado to know about possibly disastrous Earth changes these days. All you need to do is follow the news and the science. The effects of global climate change, whether you attribute it to human-caused global warming or natural phenomena, like solar flares or cyclic changes, are real and are affecting all life on earth. A recent two-hour special on the National Geographic Channel called "Six Degrees" illustrated how, as Earth's average temperature warms degree by degree, life on Earth will change, and it's not a pretty picture for humans or other species. The urgency of this message is finally getting out through the mass media and making it to the agendas of world leaders in every sector.

Think about the extreme weather patterns you have experienced in your own area just in the last year. Here in central North Carolina, after spring rains we're still deep into a prolonged drought. High winds swept through in January, causing fires that burned over 10,000 acres. That's unheard of around here. In addition, temperatures from spring to fall last year were hotter than usual. Weeks passed when the day time temperatures didn't dip below 90 degrees. In early June this year we had several days of 100+ degree temperatures. Those without air conditioning suffered greatly. Remember the 30,000 or more who died in Europe a few years back from a relentless heat wave? When people, animals and plant life experience sudden or prolonged periods of severe climate change, disruption of life as we know it is going to happen.

The two great natural disasters of 2004-2005, the Asian tsunami and Hurricane Katrina, which occurred within eight months of each other, wiped out hundreds of thousands of people, let alone other species, and billions of financial assets.

Recently my family and I watched a program on the History Channel called "Last Days on Earth." Programs like this are popping up all over, placing scenarios before us that are possible or even probable, although when they might happen is usually vague. This program detailed the seven most likely disasters which could end human life on Earth. In ascending order of importance, they were: 7) the death of a star, causing either intense gamma ray bursts that roast the planet or wandering black holes that suck us up; 6) Technology so intelligent that it destroys the human race (remember Hal the Computer in the movie *2001: A Space Odyssey* ?);

5) a supervolcano, like the caldera filled with molten magma under Yellowstone, that erupts and wipes out life across the Earth; 4) an asteroid or near-Earth object, like the one scheduled to pass Earth on April 13, 2009 and pass again closer seven years later; 3) a nuclear explosion, either intentional or accidental; 2) pandemics or plagues; or 1) climate changes of the kind we're already experiencing. The only one of these that wasn't on my own list was number 6. But it isn't difficult to imagine that intelligent technology could overtake human intelligence, representing the triumph of the mind over the heart. Note that human factors and causes could account at least in part for number 6 and the final three disasters.

Without reciting any more of this litany of possible disasters, I'd like to focus on those natural ones that are part of the 2012 predictions. The most significant and potentially disruptive of these are a pole shift and increased earthquake and solar flare activity.

From time to time in the history of the Earth, its magnetic poles have slipped and reversed. The two key signs that move a pole shift from the possible to the probable are sudden climate change and weakening of Earth's electromagnetic fields. Mainstream publications like *The New York Times* and *Scientific American* have published data in the last few years indicating that these two signs are much in evidence. Electromagnetic fields are weakening all over the planet, and the weakest are found on the west coast of the United States and the area of the Middle East from the Suez Canal into Israel. Interestingly, as Gregg Braden, author of *The God Code* and other books, has observed, these areas are less stable than places with strong magnetic energy, like Russia for example, and therefore more volatile not only geologically but also politically and culturally. The weaker the field, the more open the humans in the area are to change, and the reverse is also true.

One source has suggested that a pole shift will result in Earth losing its tilt to become vertical, while the moon slips relative to the Earth and through gravitational pull causes the oceans to cover the east and west coasts of North and South America for at least twenty-five miles inland from the current boundaries. Other extreme Earth changes would also result. There is scientific evidence for what has happened in the past when poles shifted. Will it happen by 2012? Is this the great cataclysm predicted in Doomsday scenarios?

In addition, Earth is bombarded periodically by cycles of solar storms. Solar rain expert Mitch Batros follows these carefully on his website, www.earthchangesmedia.com. A new cycle is underway, expected to be up to 50% stronger than past cycles and to peak in 2011-2012. These storms will bombard us with charged solar particles and contribute to more frequent and severe earthquakes, hurricanes, snowstorms, tornadoes, and volcanic eruptions. This increased solar activity will disrupt human electromagnetic fields just as it has already disrupted the migratory patterns of birds, whales, and dolphins. Physical and mental illness and disorientation are likely outcomes.

The combination of weakening electromagnetic fields and strengthening solar flare activity are significant enough, but add to this the lining up of the Earth, Sun, and Galactic Center on Winter Solstice, 2012, and you have the makings for the most dramatic Earth changes since the disappearance of the dinosaur. According to astrologists and others who have followed closely the movements of the planets in our solar system, Earth already has entered into the photon belt associated with the galactic alignment. This belt of highly charged light particles or photons could contribute to the disruption of electromagnetic fields. Some believe photons will peak in 2012, resulting in an energetic burst that will boost the shift to higher consciousness or possibly create havoc on Earth—or both.

Some of these scenarios are more probable than others, backed by science as well as ancient beliefs and traditions. What could any one of these or a combination of them mean for the human race and other life on Earth? At one extreme is the possibility of mass extinction—billions of lives lost, large portions of the Earth becoming uninhabitable, and the end of life as we know it. Earth herself will recover, just without most of her human and animal population. Not long ago I watched an eerie program on the History Channel: "Life After People." It showed graphically the principle of entropy, how Earth would adapt over time and reclaim land given over for human purposes until no human traces remained. Even more interesting was my visit to this program's website, which included a survival guide should a catastrophe occur and a chat site, where viewers made comments. The National Geographic Channel aired the same program as "Aftermath: Life After People." I believe both of these programs were based on Alan Weisman's 2007 best seller, *The World Without Us*. Information on all of these is available on the internet. Together, these sources paint a bleak picture of the future for the human species.

It is possible that humanity and other species could survive a pole shift, intense solar activity or other mass extinction event. For most people, contemplating such a scenario brings up intense fear. Barbara Hand Clow in her book *Catastrophia* suggests that such fear is based on memories of past such events in the collective subconscious. Fear is our worst enemy, so when we feel it coming up we need to breathe deeply and release it. We'll look more closely at possible future scenarios a bit later and ways to prepare for each of these.

So Earth can survive without humans, but humans can't survive without the Earth—unless life is carried to the stars where it may either survive in another form or on a compatible planet. I recently caught part of an old "Twilight Zone" episode in which a colony of people survived on another planet for thirty years. Eventually a space ship from "home" arrived to rescue them, but the colony's leader sabotaged the return in order to remain in control of "his" people. A common theme in science fiction is that human consciousness hasn't kept up with advances in technology. It's the old head over heart conflict that we've got to get past as we move toward Unity Consciousness.

In addition to all the possible Earth changes we're facing on our way to 2012 and beyond are those caused or contributed to by humans, for better or for worse. The brilliant physicist Stephen Hawking believes that these are more likely than the natural Earth changes, but I think we're going to see a combination of them. As the time for the Great Shift approaches ever more swiftly, the forces that are not ready for an enlightened humanity are acting out their death throes. While World War II was our parents' or grandparents' war, and those of us in the allied nations who lived through it believed it was necessary to stop genocide, the legacy of nuclear war falls squarely on my generation's side of the ledger. My husband, Alden, worked for several years for Dr. James Conant, an eminent scientist and president of Harvard University, who became one of the chief architects of the Manhattan Project. Alden assisted Dr. Conant in his studies of American schools at the time of Sputnik. A deeply moral man, Conant always felt a degree of guilt for his part—humanity's part—in developing the first weapon of mass destruction. In later years he fought hard for international control of atomic energy.

While control measures have been taken, nuclear weapons are now in the hands of the so-called "rogue" nations, like Iran and North Korea, and the scenario of a nuclear holocaust remains possible. I remember the Barry Goldwater vs. L .B. Johnson election of 1964, when the Johnson campaign effectively convinced the public that Goldwater wouldn't hesitate to use nuclear weapons through an ad showing a mushroom cloud exploding in the background while an innocent little girl picked flowers in a field. The Bush administration's invasion of Iraq under the guise of eliminating an evil dictator with weapons of mass destruction has been exposed for the misguided tragedy that it is, during which tens of thousands have died without an end in sight. One huge lesson which a growing majority of people surely have gotten from the Iraq war is that one nation has no right to impose on another its ideology or its voracious need for that nation's natural resources. Democracies cannot be imposed on people who have never experienced them. They must choose an empowering government and learn through experience how to make it work. Wise, spiritually mature leaders are in short supply in today's world. Yet there are signs of hope.

I find it very interesting that Senator Barack Obama has a good chance of becoming the next U.S. president. As one media commentator put it, Obama is a Rorschach test for people's psyches. They see themselves in him. Son of a Kenyan agnostic Muslim father and an Anglo mother (whose last name, Dunham, I share!), Obama grew up in the Pacific Ocean polyglot cultures of Hawaii and Indonesia and, after Harvard Law School, worked for nonprofits engaged in social justice. He's an image of America as melting pot, of living out the American Dream of freedom and possibility. While he still has one foot in old paradigm politics in the U.S. senate, at 46 he's attracting a wide variety of supporters, including the Kennedys, who believes he can inspire the American public in the same way JFK did. Whether he does or not remains to be seen, but he is the kind of new leader who potentially can bring out the best in this American nation that has lost its way.

In addition to wars and conflicts large and small based on limited, old paradigm belief systems and the kind of human-caused ecological disaster we have already glimpsed—depletion of natural resources such as water, oil, and forests, pollution of our waters, lands, and skies, mass extinction of species caused by development, overpopulation, global warming and so forth—another potential disaster on the road to 2012 centers around the global economy. All of these problems are, of course, linked as part of the interconnected systems we spoke of earlier. Signs are present that a worldwide financial collapse could be imminent, triggered by the housing and credit crises in the U.S. The bubble has burst on the inflationary housing market, and in most areas of the country housing is in steep decline. People are losing their equity in their homes, their future wealth. The situation has gone well beyond a market "correction."

Hundreds of thousands of people can't sell their homes, can't move to find new jobs, and can't draw out home equity to carry them through a crisis. A couple of years ago Michigan considered itself in a one-state recession. Now, it looks as though the rest of the nation is joining in.

The subprime mortgage debacle, in which people without sufficient income and assets were encouraged to take on mortgages beyond their means, has already caused massive defaults and foreclosures around the country, and the Federal Reserve is now regularly bailing out huge financial conglomerates like Bank of America, Citibank, and Bear Stearns with overnight loans to meet cash demands. The largest U.S. mortgage lender, Countrywide, which holds the mortgage on our own home, is nearly bankrupt, and its acquisition by cash-strapped Bank of America is unlikely to rescue the situation.

Anyone who travels abroad is aware of the collapse of the American dollar against foreign currencies, and nations like China and India, whose economies have exploded in recent years, find that their stock markets move in tandem with the U.S. markets in this linked global economy. If the U.S. dollar is replaced by the Euro or gold bullion as the standard of international exchange, and if Asian nations stop purchasing our bonds, another worldwide depression is likely. Even though other major world economies like China, Russia, and Brazil may be strong, they will still be adversely impacted by a long term downtrend in the U.S. Our astronomical national debt, fueled by war and tax cuts, has depleted our treasury and reduced our options, no matter how fast and furiously our treasury prints new money.

I was a Certified Financial Planner for twenty-one years in private practice and later in ministry in the church. In my business, my task was to help people make the best use of their financial resources to meet their stated goals, and in the ministry to help them look at the spirituality of money and make wise choices about what they would spend, save for future needs, and give to charity. Financial security is essential to people's sense of wellbeing and most have no greater material attachment than their money. Therefore, the threat of a financial collapse is scarier to them than anything else I've mentioned so far, and it's also very possible, even probable.

One of the big lessons each of us has to learn as we approach 2012 and prepare ourselves for the Great Shift is to release our fear and anxiety about money. That fear in essence is about not having enough, a perceived lack of abundance, tied to a diminished sense of confidence that the Universe will provide whatever we need. This fear is deepest for those who accumulate more and more material possessions and wealth, as though if they continue to do so they will eventually have enough, although most couldn't tell you how much is enough. The more they have the more they may believe they are entitled to or deserve. In my experience, those who live from day to day are actually more likely to trust in God or the Universe to sustain them and to be grateful for what they have received.

In the spiritual life, humility and gratitude are paramount. If we can learn to be grateful for everything, even our greatest challenges in life, then we're well on our way to higher dimension consciousness. Heart-felt gratitude in all things is built upon trust in and alignment with a Higher Power, the God of our understanding.

In the event of a financial collapse, a huge wave of fear among humans will release, greater than the Asian tsunami and more far-reaching. We will need all of our spiritual resources and determination to stay centered in our hearts and not be sucked into the fear. As we resonate with a higher frequency emotion, the vibration of love, we can help pull up others with us rather than be dragged down to lower emotions.

In Chapter Seven we'll look at how to prepare for what may become a money-free future in which people within their communities have enough both through a reduction in perceived need and the sharing of resources. In the higher consciousness, resources are no longer hoarded by the few. Those who through their religious institutions or compassionate hearts have had experience with giving extravagantly out of a sense of abundance rather than sparingly or grudgingly out of a sense of lack will be our role models in this dimension of the coming shift.

My own book, *Graceful Living: Your Faith, Values, and Money in Changing Times*, has been a text on this subject. The book was commissioned by the Ecumenical Stewardship Center, an organization of twenty-seven Christian denominations in the U.S. and Canada, to help church members deal with their money issues in ways that free them from old patterns and help them discover how much is enough—the key question, I believe, for the over-consuming American population. We are likely to revise our sense of what is enough after moving through the changes that are coming.

So war and conflict, ecological disasters, and a financial collapse are the main human-caused or human-exacerbated possibilities already in our way on the path to 2012. We'll do well to dodge any of these. The consequences of one or more of them include immense suffering and loss on the parts of whole populations of the human, animal, plant, and mineral kin-doms. Now you can see what needs to be overcome in time for Earth and her inhabitants to make it through to a higher order of being. It will take all spiritually awakened people creating more positive visions of the future to divert us from our collision course with disaster.

CHAPTER THREE: FIVE SCENARIOS ON THE WAY TO 2012

The Epiphany Weekend Conversation

On Epiphany Weekend, January 5-6, 2008, I gathered sixteen experienced spiritual healers and teachers at my home for a conversation about the coming Great Shift. I called it "Five Years and Counting: The Path to 2012 and Beyond." The invitation was extended to those who have been engaged for years in spiritual service as well as in their own inner work of clearing and releasing old, stuck patterns and harmonizing and balancing their energies to be able to hold a high energetic vibration and attune to the higher realms of consciousness. I wanted to know what they believed, discerned, and expected would happen in the years leading to and following 2012 and what roles each of them and all of us together were guided to play for the highest good of the Earth and the Universe.

Epiphany, which commemorates the visitation to the infant Jesus by the three wise men, the Magi, seemed an especially appropriate time for such a conversation. To me it symbolized the gathering of wise spiritual leaders who recognized then and now that the Christ Consciousness has been birthed into human form. Two thousand years ago it came for the first time, and the Christ presented the pattern, the blueprint, for all humanity to ascend into a higher dimension of consciousness and being. Now our gathering symbolized the wise ones of our own time tapping into the Christ or Unity Consciousness to assist human ascension, in effect becoming part of the same pattern.

For two days we shared our own knowledge, experience, and insights about what may be coming and how to prepare for the kinds of changes described in the previous chapter. We had many "epiphanies" or spiritually guided insights into what lies ahead and our own parts in the upcoming drama. Most of us knew each other from our work as spiritual energy healers and teachers with Arcing Light and other healing modalities. Five men and eleven women ranging in age from 38 to 70 attended from four states and across North Carolina. A number of us have traveled together at our own expense to places like Egypt, Panama, Scotland, and Mayan Mexico to offer Earth healing and soul clearing at sacred sites, power points, and other locations to which we were guided. We have worked together in many kinds of situations to shift energy to higher levels to benefit people, places, and the planet, even preventing, we believe, a specifically targeted attack on a site in the U.S. Forming groups that come together for particular tasks and assignments to which we feel guided, we are energetically connected not only with each other through our hearts and our work but also with others around the world. We have built community with each other and networked with like-minded people in many places.

This was a powerful, harmonized group of spiritual leaders gathered on Epiphany Weekend, and it was time to talk and discern together our responses to the coming shift. My impression before the meeting was that everyone was aware of what might happen between now and 2012 and was working hard to prepare mentally, emotionally, and spiritually for the higher dimension consciousness we were already experiencing, but that most of us hadn't considered in any detail the physical details and logistics of getting to 2012. We agreed that it was time to begin that conversation.

We started with the major questions each of us was bringing to the conversation and the list of topics we wanted to cover, given below:

- What we can do to make the shift more loving and peaceful

- The importance of staying in the heart in the vibration of love and not going into fear
- The importance of taking positive, appropriate action as well as opening the heart
- How not to contribute through our thoughts and actions to the severity of the shift
- How to connect with other realms and like-minded groups assisting the shift
- The importance of developing intentional, sustainable community
- How to include others in the conversation, especially those not aware of or prepared for the coming changes
- Our responsibility to others as we move through the shift
- How to make preparing for the shift our primary occupation

These topics indicated what was on our minds as we entered the conversation. It soon became even more wide-ranging. We reviewed and updated everyone on the major prophecies and predictions given in Chapter Two and agreed that the preponderance of evidence is that 2012, give or take a year or two, is likely to mark the Great Shift in consciousness that is already underway. Agreeing that the Mayan calendar is one of the most convincing signs, we noted that we have been working for years to help bring about this shift and are experiencing its early effects through our own processes of cleansing and releasing old, stuck energy and thought forms from ourselves, others, and the Earth, using spiritual practices daily that keep us in alignment with Spirit and occasionally exchanging healing sessions with each other to stay balanced.

No matter how far people are along their spiritual paths, they always have more to learn and more to clear. When we find ourselves getting irritated at others, it is often because they are mirroring something to us that we need to work on in ourselves. That happens within our families and communities even when we have the best of intentions. Part of what helps us clear out negative energy is recognizing how we participate in keeping it alive. One way we know we're entering the expanded Unity Consciousness is that we recognize what we're doing and shift the pattern with our intention and our love. Spiritual energy healing work, in my experience, can help shift these patterns more quickly than anything else. I'm grateful for my healer friends who have often helped me release and realign.

In discussing the major prophecies and predictions concerning 2012, one of our group mentioned that many religious conservatives also anticipate the end of the world as we know it and believe in preparing for the end times. The popular *Left Behind* series of the '90's, which I personally found misguided and harmful, is an example. We noted that the Great Shift presents an opportunity for humankind and the whole planet to evolve or ascend to an expanded way of being, the higher vibration Unity Consciousness, whereas the Doomsday scenarios paint dire pictures of "sinners" roasting in hell. The assumption is that "we" will survive and ascend, while "they" will perish.

The Great Shift is not about judgment or creating fear in people, but rather about the healing power of love, Divine Love, which is all inclusive. No one is left behind. All are offered access to higher dimension consciousness. Yes, we must choose that love, but Divine Love offers itself to us over and over until we understand and choose. In this age when the Divine Feminine is everywhere enveloping the world in her compassionate, nurturing energy, more and more people are coming into balance. Together we can choose a kinder, gentler future, not a harsher one.

Just a moment ago, on my lunch break, I read an article in *USA Today* about the shift in people's attitudes toward animal rights. I see this as part of what is already changing for the better. For years I've been passionate about the treatment of animals, when to many my views seemed extreme. In a sermon I preached in 1996 in a church I was serving in the South, I explained why I was at the time a vegetarian. Many in the congregation had expressed curiosity about that, as it was unusual to them. I felt that the abuse and neglect of animals, particularly those God had placed in our care or that we had chosen as our companions, reflected human ignorance, and said that factory farming was one of the worst of these abuses we all participated in by eating meat. There was more, but you get the picture. It was a consciousness-raising moment on both sides. A number in the congregation found my views offensive and "not biblical". I realized I could have been more diplomatic in my expressions of the place of animals in the creation. As time went on, several people remembered to bring vegetarian dishes to our occasional potluck suppers, and I could see that even though some people were riled up by that sermon it was having a positive effect.

The *USA Today* article mentioned three events in recent years that had raised people's awareness about the plight of animals and caused new legislation and initiatives to bring about positive change. The first was Hurricane Katrina, when thousands lost their companion and domestic animals because there were no evacuation plans for them. The other two, news making events of 2007, were the revolting dog fighting expose connected with Michael Vick, the NFL player, and the pet food recall after thousands of pets were poisoned by poor quality imported food. What these three events demonstrate is how the negative is balanced out by the positive and how consciousness shifts. Hearts are opened by loving, compassionate responses. There was righteous anger involved also that prompted social action.

Keep in mind as we approach 2012 that in the midst of the harshest and darkest of events, love will be present and guiding us through. Love is the balance, the redemptive power that keeps all of the Earth- and human-caused changes in perspective. Trusting this and surrendering our limited understanding and the need to control to the Higher Consciousness of Love will see us through whatever is in our path on the way to 2012 and beyond. Our conversation group tried always to keep this perspective in front of us as we considered what is coming.

The group talked about how to communicate with those holding the Doomsday consciousness and, indeed, with anyone who has limited awareness of the coming shift. It was a topic we returned to several times, as we recognized that proselytizing is not the way, and that speaking from our own experiences, telling our own stories, speaking the truth as we understand it with love, is more effective. If we connect with people on a heart level and don't try to win arguments or wear them down with what we perceive as superior knowledge and wisdom, we'll have a better chance of helping them understand while learning something ourselves and together taking the steps necessary to prepare for the coming transformation.

Building bridges and relationships will assist the movement into Unity Consciousness. We want everyone to be a part of it, not just the so-called "enlightened" ones. Serving the Light means seeing from the higher perspective of the eagle in flight and holding in love and light the highest good of all. Those in our group didn't want to be perceived as a cult or a fringe group with weird ideas. Most of us are pretty mainstream with our lives and work and are good communicators. As one person suggested, it's good to "warm your thoughts through your heart before you speak", quoting Rudolph Steiner, the well-known scientist and metaphysician.

We noted that the myths of many cultures include a consciousness of discontinuity with the past and a desire to return to a previous, more pristine time of perfection, like Adam and Eve returning to the Garden of Eden. 2012 is not about returning to the past but rather of merging with the future, co-creating it with the Divine power of Love.

Another prediction came up that must be considered. Each person will go through the changes in his or her own way and at his or her own level. Those who hold the higher frequencies may either stay on Earth to create together a new future or be lifted off the Earth into another dimension, perhaps on another planet or in another star system. Those not ready for the shift are not likely to survive the changes. After passing through death, they will be taken to places prepared for them, where they can continue to evolve. There is a loving kindness in this, and I consider it a strong possibility. While these concepts may be new or surprising to some, they are consistent with many spiritual teachings. Most of us in the group had the sense that we would remain and assist others through the transition. The importance of building new kinds of communities was another topic we returned to several times and is the focus of Chapter Six.

The group shared a sense that there is no one right or wrong answer about what is to come, only possibilities and probabilities based on the signs and guidance given. Mother Earth needs to cleanse herself, and if that means that millions or billions of humans must leave, we accept that as having a higher purpose. As we talked together, we expressed our preferences for a gentler shift and commitment to doing what we can to work with Spirit for a less harsh outcome. Most of us had a sense that we elected to be here on Earth at this time to play our appointed roles, that the timing and degree of ascension is not yet known or fixed, but that it will happen soon. In that vein, an Indian teacher, Amma-ji, is said to have known that the Asian tsunami would occur in 2004 but chose not to forewarn people. She believed that the result would be a necessary heart opening, an anchoring of Divine Feminine energy, through the outpouring of love and compassion for those who were lost and left afterwards. Our work is not to preach doom and gloom but to help people open their hearts so that we will experience a softer landing. This will help balance the male/female energies as part of the shift. The action (masculine energy) we take will be based on our intuition (feminine energy). Both are needed.

There was talk about how we might communicate on a more heart-based, intuitive level after the shift. Words and language can cause misunderstanding, as in the Tower of Babel story. Telepathic communication is based on resonances between people, on their unity, not their separateness. Even now through body language and intention we can convey to people, animals, and plants a sense of safety, security, and acceptance, lessening their fright in traumatic situations.

Several of us were aware of the Hathor message mentioned in the previous chapter, along with the messages coming through from the Pleaidian star system. Both of these multidimensional group consciousnesses vibrate in resonance with Divine Love and offer useful guidance. We are becoming more aware of our multi-dimensionality ourselves—being able to connect with dimensions beyond those we associate with Earth–and are feeling less isolated in the Universe. The shift of Earth and her inhabitants is essential for the whole Universe to expand and create at ever higher and higher levels of consciousness. Humanity is holding Earth and the rest of the cosmos back with our violence and greed. By raising ourselves, we raise all. This is the nature of the interconnected web of life.

After half a day of conversation along these lines, our group was ready to outline the scenarios we thought were possible or probable in the years 2008 to 2012. It turned out there were five. I had thought of four, so the fifth was a bit of a surprise. Still, it made sense. I've listed these five below, along with what might characterize each of them.

Five Possible Scenarios on the Path to 2012 and Beyond

1. Extreme Destruction
In this scenario huge Earth changes will occur of the kind described in the previous chapter. These may include a pole shift, extreme climate change, severe drought, water wars, mass migration, massive species extinction, erosion and destruction of ecosystems, tsunamis, hurricanes and other storms, solar eruptions, volcanoes, pandemics, and other natural disasters that will change the shape

of the world. The lives of millions or billions of humans and other species will end. Some may survive.

Human-caused changes are the other possible part of this scenario. These may include worldwide war, possible use of nuclear or biological weapons, a global financial collapse, the collapse of other structures, institutions, and systems such as governments, religions, technology and communications, water systems, food production, health care, education, and so on. Some of these would result from violence, and some from the failure of old systems to adapt. Famine could be considered both a consequence of Earth changes such as drought and human causes such as overpopulation. Again, millions or billions of lives could be lost. At the least, life as we know it would end. Chaos and anarchy could replace the collapse of institutions until some sort of follow-on system takes hold.

This is the worst-case scenario. Any one or combination of these circumstances could cause massive loss of life and upheaval that would make survival difficult if not impossible. None of these is necessarily timed to happen between now and 2012, with the exception of the solar storm activity that is expected to create more extreme weather, but all are within the realm of possibility. Some pieces of this scenario have already happened or are currently happening in parts of the world.

2. Significant Changes

Major Earth and systemic changes like those named above occur in this scenario. These would not be as wide-spread or necessarily as severe. They might be more localized, although the interconnections of all systems would affect the whole. These changes might occur over several years rather than all at once, giving Earth and humanity time to recover, at least partially, between episodes. Like the Asian tsunami, the Myanmar cyclone, the China earthquake, or Hurricane Katrina, the aftermath of these calamities may teach people to open their hearts and become more compassionate and loving toward each other, other species, and the Earth. This shift in attitude could help many make the transformation to Unity Consciousness.

3. Few Changes—a Soft Landing
While major Earth and systemic changes will occur, they will not be as devastating as in the preceding scenarios. There could be either fewer changes or less severe ones. If all of us are learning our life lessons and connecting with the vibration of love, we will be able to weather the changes through helping each other. Lightworkers will work with the higher dimensions to bring about a soft landing for humanity and the whole Earth. The changes that occur will seem more natural or the result of collective efforts to bring about change.

4. No Discernable Change or Waking Up to a New World
This scenario includes two possibilities: 1) the changes that do occur will be evolutionary, happening slowly and naturally as opposed to transformative, happening suddenly, so that they take place almost without conscious recognition; or 2) the transformation will happen without our prior awareness. Everything will be set down in place by the higher dimensions, and we'll experience a Golden Age on Earth without going through the trauma.

In either case, there will be a recognition that humanity is stepping into the fullness of its potential but that is likely to be seen on the one hand as expected human progress or on the other as brought about by the higher dimensions without much human involvement.

5. All of the Above
This is the scenario I had not considered until our group brought it up. Yet it makes sense in a way. People will experience either different events or the same event differently. In recent years the Earth and her inhabitants have already begun to experience the

kinds of conditions and events mentioned in Scenario 1, but these have impacted some more directly than others. As long as what happens seems localized, people will not necessarily pay attention, or they might feel a little empathy for a time but soon return to their own concerns.

If we accept that we live in a multidimensional universe and that time is not linear, we might also accept the possibility that the different scenarios could be running in parallel and that what we experience depends on our levels of awareness and consciousness as well as our locations.

Which of these scenarios do you resonate with? I really wanted to know what the people in our group sensed and believed about what is coming, so after we had discussed these five possibilities, I asked them to take some silent time to go deep within, connect with their spiritual guides and intuition, reflect on these scenarios, and then share their perceptions and feelings with the whole group.

Spiritual Guidance and Discernment

Before revealing our conclusions, I want to return to the process of spiritual discernment mentioned at the beginning of Chapter Two. Such a process of gathering information, exploring options, reflecting and meditating is essential for making important decisions and ensuring that you are not acting hastily or without connecting with Source energy. It is about asking for inner guidance from the highest dimensions, from the Source you draw upon for what you understand to be wisdom and truth. You may experience a knowing, an energetic pull toward one or another option, or a need for further information or clarity before drawing a conclusion. All that you need, the inner voice or confirmation, is available to you. How you receive guidance depends on your innate gifts and how you develop them.

Years ago I found that my body was an energetic pendulum. I can feel when something is spiritually confirmed or not, and I get auditory messages and visual images as well. People sometimes experience what they consider a spiritual message or call to redirect their lives. I received such a call in November, 1991. It felt like an energetic download or knowing, totally unexpected but unmistakable. Yet I continued to ask for confirmation. In a dream that night I saw the words "one clear call", a phrase from the Tennyson poem "Dover Beach." The words were framed and large so that I could not miss them. Soon afterwards, in that twilight moment between sleep and awakening, I felt a strong energetic presence pin me in place. From deep within my soul I responded, "Your obedient servant, Lord" over and over. This came not from conscious awareness but from a source within me I didn't know I had. At the time I was 48 years old and had major work commitments. I dropped them to respond to what I knew was going to take me in an entirely different direction into a new kind and level of service.

There was no mistaking this "call." Whether or not anyone else felt that this summoning by Spirit was genuine, I knew that it was. Yet, I consulted others—family, friends, church leaders I trusted—because what I was being called to was so unexpected. Some were as surprised as I was, others said they were not, that this was just the next step in my lifelong spiritual quest. Within a week I had applied to seminary and begun the process that would conclude three years later with a Master of Divinity degree and a few months after that with ordination into the professional ministry and a position serving in a large church. Along the way I had to go through a group discernment process set up by the denomination to convince those in charge that I was suited and prepared for the ministry. I must say that this process was at times uncomfortable and felt like jumping through hoops. Nevertheless, I persisted.

When the message is this clear, even when it's a surprise, there is no choice but to commit and take action, regardless of the opinions of those around you. However, when the message, intuition or nudging isn't as clear or you find yourself resisting, then it can be very helpful to have a community you trust to help you process what's coming through and how to respond. This multi-layered discernment process, which may include research as well as processing within a trusted group, is particularly helpful for really important decisions. Ultimately, however, you must go within for the answer, to that deep spiritual connection within you that responds "Yes!" to the call of Spirit.

You may choose to work with a particular spiritual guide, such as one of the archangels or ascended masters, who will assist you in clarifying what you need to know and do. These days, when so many awakened people have developed ongoing relationships with these Beings of Light, messages abound on the internet, and many spiritual channelers and teachers are available for personal sessions. You will again need to discern carefully what it is you are receiving and whether or not it resonates with your inner spirit. Not everyone is a clear conduit. As mentioned earlier, we all have our own perceptions, perspectives, and filters through which information and guidance comes, and it can be highly individual. Your own discernment may lead you to different conclusions. That's okay. We don't all have to agree. We are at different points on our spiritual journeys, have different belief systems, connect with different levels of vibration or frequencies, and get our information and guidance from different sources. What we discern for ourselves through the kind of process I've described is what we have to go with, although we're continually adding new information and more guidance to refine and possibly redirect our thoughts and actions.

Remember, thought is energy and is directed by our intentions and emotions for better or for worse. If we go into fear with our thoughts, then that is what we put out into the energetic fields we all draw from. If our intention is to release fear for transmutation into light, then we assist the whole field in holding a higher vibration of trust, confidence, courage and love.

Returning to our group's discernment process about the five scenarios outlined above during Epiphany Weekend, our individual responses differed in the particulars but had a commonality to them that validated the process.

First of all, we agreed that to some extent we create our own reality, through our own thoughts, beliefs, and actions. Therefore, a major question was this: by expecting the worst do we participate in creating it? A related question was if the most extreme scenario in fact did take place, how would we view that? Would it be a disaster for the Earth? For humanity? Or would it move Earth and humanity more quickly into their own next stages of evolution? In other words, even if we discerned that Scenario 1 was the most likely, this result would also have its positive side. We would trust that things happened that way for reasons we were not aware of or privy to and that as human consciousness expands and transforms we will see a more complete picture. We do what we can to support the shift but ultimately when and how it happens is the result of many complex factors. With that understanding, we are freed from the fear, anxiety, and trauma which would accompany the first couple of scenarios and continue to contribute to raising the vibration on the planet by whatever means we can. Indeed, more will be called for from us in the second, third, and fourth scenarios than from the first. I'll explain in a moment.

Facing whatever anxiety emerges within us as we contemplate the possibilities is the first step in our preparation for whatever will come. Recognizing it, examining it, and releasing it is part of the process. To the extent we are able to do that, we are on a level of spiritual maturity that will carry us through the transition to Unity Consciousness. We hope for a soft landing but are ready for anything.

Some of the responses of our group after the silent meditation follow.

One person envisioned a back-to-nature society in which humanity once again learned to live with and off the land, understanding and being in harmony with natural processes and other species. He saw people living in small communities, growing their own food, and sharing the abundance of the Earth with respect for all life. They knew and followed natural law and lived in a manner that reflected their spiritual connection with Earth and the cosmos. This seemed like a vision of a new Eden or possibly a memory from the distant past.

Another person had a vision of a chart with a big number 1 highlighted on one side, and the numbers 2, 3, and 4 on the other. His interpretation of this was that Scenario 1 was the most likely now, but with humans working in concert with cosmic forces, it could move to 2 or lower. His sense was that all of these were still possibilities.

Several people sensed that we would each stay in our own reality and, while we would see destruction going on all around us, would not be caught up in it. We would stay in place, in a space of contentment and love, sending positive energy to the chaos around us. This part of the group felt that Scenario 2 was most likely but that what would happen would be localized. One expressed her commitment to helping take care of others when the time came and that all of us would be needed to help transmute and heal the pain others would experience during and following the changes. In this way we would contribute to helping people and the Earth shift into the vibration of love and experience Unity Consciousness.

Another member of the group sensed that significant Earth and human-caused changes would occur, somewhere between Scenarios 1 and 2. She felt that some of these had already happened or were happening—extreme climate changes, species loss, war, financial collapse and so on—and that these would increase until the shift happens.

One person who has spent years preparing for the physical changes expected during the Great Shift felt that although there would be some destruction, a soft landing was likely because of all the work awakened, conscious people had done and were doing to bring that about. She and her family had prepared space on their large farm that could house and provide for dozens, perhaps even hundreds, of people short-term after a disaster of some kind. They had stockpiled food, water, seeds, homeopathic remedies, and other basic materials to ensure survival. They had horses for transportation, an extensive garden, and lived off the grid. These years of simple living and preparation offered a sanctuary that might well be needed in the future if Scenario 2 or 3 came to pass. In her mind's eye she saw symbols of transformation and was given the understanding that those of us who are aware of these possibilities are here to help bring about the shift and assist others going through their own transitions to a higher consciousness. An essential part of her vision and plan was teaching others how to prepare and presenting a viable model for them that involved living in harmony with the land and Earth's other kin-doms. She also asked the important question, "If there's going to be a soft landing, do we have to work so hard?" At some level she was feeling the burden of these years of preparation and expectation of something like Scenario 2. Would the shift to the Unity Consciousness really be so difficult, she wondered, or would we enjoy a smoother transition?

A computer designer in the group pointed out that when all the predictions were floating around about Y2K, the millennium bug or the Year 2000 Problem, there was worldwide concern that government, banking, and other major institutional computer systems would break down as the new millennium dawned because existing computer programs had failed to anticipate the year 2000. When the date passed with few problems, debate centered around whether all the efforts made to avert the problem had worked or whether the dimensions of the problem were overstated. The computer expert in our group had personally worked hard during that period on the Y2K problem and felt that the efforts put in had averted a significant systemic breakdown.

This example provided a helpful analogy in our discussion in response to the earlier question about whether our human-cosmic teams needed to work so hard to head off catastrophe and bring about a less traumatic transition through 2012. At this point, no one felt that we should let up in our work of holding the highest possible intention for a positive outcome for the Earth and her inhabitants. Besides, the Y2K threat was minimal compared to predictions and prophecies about 2012, particularly in light of the completion of the Long Count of the Mayan calendar and the conjunction of so many other long-standing expectations about the coming Great Shift.

All the messages we were getting from our guides in other dimensions were stressing the importance of our efforts as Lightworkers to support a positive outcome. We are co-creators, helping to ground high vibration energy on Earth to ensure that life continues in a way that reflects Divine Love. Yes, we have to work hard, we agreed, but not necessarily at the level of physical survival. We would revisit this question later in the gathering.

One of several world travelers in our group felt that Scenario 2 was the most likely. She had the sense that travel as we know it would end soon, and that if we wanted to see the world as it is now, we should travel in the next year or two. This resonated with several of us who frequently travel the world offering Earth healings and soul clearings (assisting the dead or stuck energetic beings to move on), along with anchoring the spiritual energy of Arcing Light at the locations to which we travel.

As we go through the Earth changes, there are likely to be limitations on our capacity to travel, at least in conventional time and space. This is currently being confirmed as airlines cut back on flights and people curtail their driving because of spiraling oil prices. Other higher-dimensional forms of travel may become part of our future, involving taking our consciousness into places we wish to visit through such means as remote viewing (connecting our consciousness with another location or person and "seeing" what's going on) and teleportation (moving not only our consciousness but our physical form to another location). A few in our group have already experienced these methods, which can be learned and enabled as we expand our consciousness and develop our capacities.

The subject of location was raised by several people. Where do we need to be when the Great Shift happens? Half a dozen in our group had moved in the past five years and felt guided to the areas where they now live in order to create the kind of space and work that would assist Earth's and humanity's ascension into higher consciousness. Others felt that they might be called to move again in the next few years to places they were needed. When Spirit calls, we must be ready to go, was the consensus. This took into account the possibility of Earth changes and systemic breakdowns that could make where we live uninhabitable or less desirable. "Be sure you are where you are supposed to be", said one person, expressing the sentiments of the group. And knowing where you are supposed to be means being in touch with your guidance at all times. If something prompts you to leave home, even temporarily, listen to that. It may be an intuitive, spiritually-guided message to be somewhere safer or where your energy is needed more than where you are now.

I recently saw an article about being just where you're supposed to be at all times. When you miss a plane or get stuck in traffic and are late for an engagement or decide to stay home rather than going out one evening, it may be because something unpleasant might have happened if you had followed through with your plans or that something good happened instead. We've all heard stories about people who were supposed to be at work at the World Trade Center on September 11, 2001, and didn't get there for one reason or another. Their lives were spared as a result. Although most abrupt changes in plans are, thankfully, not this dramatic, we need to learn to stay tuned to our guidance. While driving, have you ever instinctively turned into another lane or slowed down just before an accident occurred ahead of you? Maybe your angels were looking out for you. The more we see such synchronicities as a part of life and pay attention to them, the better off we'll be. In higher dimension consciousness, we'll be naturally aware of danger or opportunity and make adjustments easily.

One person in the group felt that more important than whatever scenario was about to happen was staying centered in his heart, maintaining a calm and peaceful center, and carrying it with him whatever the situation. He echoed the sentiments of everyone. We can work from wherever we are, wherever we are meant to be, whether it is here on Earth or on the other side of death. As we hear that and resonate with it, it deepens our trust in the ultimate outcome.

Just as several people had sensed that chaos and destruction might be going on around them but that they would be all right, one woman had a vision of being transported to a beautiful white light, where she received the message, "It depends on you." She could see a counter moving backwards and forwards, as though how we respond and what we do is impacting even now the outcome. She sensed, as others had, that if we are the expression of the love we are we will experience the shift as in Scenario 4, as though it barely happened, as though it is a continuity of lives well lived in alignment with Spirit.

This healer and teacher also had visions of creating a space of love in and around her home, including gardens that would supply nourishing food. Her vision was a confirmation that staying in the love energy is essential for each and all of us. Those who do will be supported at that level.

A couple of others also felt that creating gardens and growing our own food was an important part of the pre- and post-2012 world. Living in small communities and sharing this effort as well as the produce was mentioned by several in their reflections on what is to come. Much more is covered on this topic in Chapter Eight.

Another of our visionary members, a shaman-healer-teacher, received highly symbolic visual images: a vortex in the ocean, a food fight in a cafeteria, running from a doctor with a needle, canning food in her kitchen, and practicing archery in her back yard. These symbolic images suggested to her and the rest of the group that there would be destruction and devastation involving the ocean, food shortages, possibly a pandemic, but that, again, tending our gardens, returning to a harmonious relationship with the natural world, harvesting what nature provides for us, and staying centered in our own space would be the best strategy as things change around us.

Another person in our group had a vision of standing at home looking out the windows, watching waves of water reaching the house and not getting upset. The message she received is to aim for the 4th scenario, to know that we are spiritual masters and are supported by angels and other realms. Like several others, she viewed devastation happening around her but saw herself standing in the midst of it and helping others through it.

One person sensed that a natural disaster like an asteroid or a human-caused event like a financial collapse would happen at some point and that those who survived would return to a simpler, more agrarian form of society.

Someone else chose Scenario 5 and pointed out that all of the other four scenarios were happening now. We agreed that what we experience depends not only where we are physically but also on our perspectives.

That prompted me to observe that if you use the image of the spiral as the metaphor for perspective, we could experience changes as severe as those in Scenario 2 while perceiving them from the next highest perspective as Scenario 3. I think that's what a number in our group were doing as they envisioned devastation and chaos happening around them but maintained a calm, peaceful, loving center in the face of these events.

I have my own particular ways of asking my guidance for clarity. I asked on two different occasions and both times received the confirmation that Scenario 3, the soft landing, was the most likely as of now. I sensed that Scenario 2 would happen for many around the world but that the third option was the way those coming into Unity Consciousness would experience and perceive it. That, finally, was the consensus of the group and emphasized the importance of our being spiritually, emotionally, mentally, and physically prepared for what was to come.

Throughout this part of the conversation on which of the five scenarios seemed most likely, several other helpful observations were made. One was that what we fear most is what we draw to us. Being fearful about what is coming will draw us into more destruction, not just as individuals but as the whole of humanity. I noted that we can learn from the examples of spiritual leaders like Jesus, Gandhi, and Martin Luther King, Jr., who practiced nonviolent direct action in the face of violence. Offer no resistance, roll with the punches, turn the other cheek, and continue to be the love that you are. Potentially violent situations can be handled this way. That strategy works because the vibration of love is so much higher than that of fear and anger. The higher vibration energy, if held long enough and amplified by a group that is spiritually connected and aligned, can raise the lower vibration toward its level. This is really what our work is about—raising the vibrations of ourselves, those around us, and the whole planet to the vibration of love, bringing us into resonance with each other, with Spirit, and thereby becoming Unity Consciousness.

Even if one of the milder scenarios, 3 or 4, results by 2012, it doesn't mean that preparation for any of them projects negativity. Preparation reduces fear and helps us stay centered. We are encouraged to prepare as we see fit, in consultation with our guidance, and to know that we are supported by other realms as well as by communities we will form around us. When we ask for assistance from other realms on Earth and in other dimensions we should be specific about what we need in the way of resources in order to eliminate misunderstandings.

One in our group, a corporate marketer, suggested that we look at these realms as our corporate sponsors who will make available to us all that we need to serve in the ways we are being asked to do. Having enough resources was an issue for several who were guided to travel to other countries to offer Earth healing. When funds are scarce we have to be more creative about how to do the work with less or to attract more. Perhaps in the future private donations will become available to those of us who do this work. Keeping a sense of gratitude for all the support we receive strengthens us.

In addition, our group felt strongly that the conversation we were having needs to spread to others so people know their actions as well as their good intentions are needed to help bring about the soft landing. Our task is to branch out of our small communities and think and act more widely and influentially now, while there is still time. Using the power of the internet to disseminate information, provide support, and network with like-minded groups is an important strategy. The group felt that being more open about who we are and what we are doing means working through any fear that might entail, such as that certain individuals or organizations could try to discredit or harm those who share the views we express.

After processing the conversation about the five scenarios, the larger group split into smaller ones for further discussion. When we met again, after lunch and a walk outside on a beautiful day to connect with nature, we revisited several of the earlier topics in more detail.

I had initiated this conversation because I sensed that while this group of healers and teachers was preparing for an anticipated spiritual transformation that might coincide with the year 2012, none of us had a very clear sense of how we would get there, what it would be like, and what challenges we might encounter along the way. We were all doing our own work–clearing, releasing, and staying centered in a place of love and high intent, while offering healing and spiritual development to others. With a couple of exceptions, we weren't doing much else to prepare for the kind of physical changes we had just discussed.

We also speculated about changes in physical form we might anticipate. As we evolve from homo sapiens to homo luminous, do we become Beings of Light like the ones we communicate with in other dimensions, no longer restricted by space and time? When the transformation comes to a higher dimension, will we still be on Earth in physical bodies or light bodies? If in light bodies, what will we need in the way of food, drink, and shelter to sustain us? If we're no longer in 3D, then we don't need to do the physical preparation we were talking about. What about those who are left in physical form? Will they survive? How? These were some of the reflections we shared together and could only discuss among like-minded people who don't claim to have all the answers. We also concluded that it doesn't matter whether any of us survived individually as long as we play our parts while here to assist Earth's and humanity's ascension into higher dimension consciousness.

My own expectation is that physical and spiritual events will propel us into a more enlightened state of being on Planet Earth. My sense is that we had gathered together and were having this conversation because we signed on before we came into this life to see Earth and humanity through these transitions before moving into any other dimension ourselves. I believe that we have a great deal more to do in 3D between now and the rapidly approaching shift. While there is much energy held around specific dates in 2011 to 2013, especially Winter Solstice, 2012, any of the five scenarios could happen either before or after those dates. 2012 thus becomes a metaphor for the Great Shift that is already happening, relieving the weight of expectation that something significant will occur on one specific day. Maybe it will, but that doesn't negate all the other changes that are going on around us.

Starting from this group's consensus about Scenarios 2 and 3—that 2 is more likely now but that we will work toward 3—our conversation shifted to a more task-oriented approach to the coming changes. How can enlightened humans co-create with the spiritual realms a smooth transition for Earth and her inhabitants? This is the key question that will be addressed in Part II: Prepare for the Great Shift.

I am grateful to this group of spiritual healers, teachers, and friends for sharing at a very deep level over the course of our two-day conversation and afterwards. Their insights, commitment, and courage confirmed that there is much strength and support to draw upon as we move along the path to 2012 and beyond. This was the first of many such conversations I hope to have with all kinds of groups as this book finds its audience. Continuing and widening this conversation is essential and is the subject of the final chapter. Equipped with an understanding of our possible and probable futures, it's time to begin our preparation.

PART II: PREPARE FOR THE GREAT SHIFT

CHAPTER FOUR: ENVISION A NEW WAY OF BEING

Start with the Intended Outcomes

During my first career in higher education, I worked for a time at a state college without walls for adults who wanted to earn a degree to enhance their careers or for personal satisfaction. This college found innovative yet rigorous ways to recognize and credential learning however and wherever it occurred: in the classroom, the work place or the school of life. The process, now widely used in education, focuses first on the desired outcomes of a course or program–knowledge and competencies–rather than content. Whether the subject is literature or biochemistry, the instructor or credentialing institution determines what the student must know and be able to do as a result of the learning experience. If students can demonstrate that they know and can do what's required, there's no need to sit in a classroom to learn in the traditional way. It took quite a shift in thinking on the part of many of the faculty we worked with back then to focus on the outcomes rather than the input.

The end result of the Great Shift and the movement through 2012 is not as easy to define as that of a college course, since it's still largely unknown. However, the intended outcome many of us hold for Earth and her inhabitants is to move through the Great Shift to the Unity Consciousness with grace and ease. That's why I'm writing this book, after all! So let's begin this section with the central question: what knowledge and wisdom will be needed for the coming years? We'll focus on four specific areas in the next chapters: discovering and strengthening your spiritual connection (Chapter Five), getting ready for a range of possible disruptions in your life and choosing your location and lifestyle (Chapter Six), preparing for and thriving in a new kind of local and global economy (Chapter Seven), and creating intentional, sustainable community (Chapter Eight). Each of these areas will require all the knowledge, skills, and wisdom we and our partners in co-creating the future can muster! The final two chapters of the book, on developing your action plan (Chapter Nine) and widening the conversation about what lies ahead and how to prepare for the most probable scenarios (Chapter Ten), concern how we take what we have learned out into the world.

In the next few years human beings will experience a great adventure, like explorers of the unknown. How do you suppose the great seafaring explorers like Columbus or Magellan felt when they sailed off into uncharted waters? Filled with excitement and a bit of trepidation? Their maps were inadequate, their navigation equipment primitive, but nonetheless they made it to new worlds–although not necessarily the ones they envisioned. They had ideas and intuition about finding new lands and new routes across the pathways of the seas. Although their access to existing knowledge was limited, they trusted their own gut instincts and enlisted support for their voyages from their royal sponsors, with high hopes of wealth and adventure. The astronauts who explored outer space and carried a vision of the future to the moon were their modern counterparts.

That's one kind of explorer, the kind history books extol, who captures the human imagination and thirst for adventure. But there is another kind as well: men and women who explore the unknown not through outer space but inner space, unlocking mysteries and accessing knowledge and wisdom well beyond the confines of our small planet. These are cosmic adventurers whose imaginations and insights venture out to the stars and beyond to the galaxies invisible to the naked eye yet visible through their inner connections to the higher dimensions. Philosophers, artists, scientists, and mystics like Pythagoras, the Pharaoh Akhenaton, Plato, Leonardo DaVinci, Theresa of Avila, and Galileo are just a few of those historical figures who explored inner space and co-created with the higher realms the pathways we follow today as our consciousness expands both inward and outward ever closer to a union with Spirit.

We need to be both kinds of explorers today, venturing into the unknown on the physical planet and cosmos and the unknown within ourselves. It will take courage as we face a future potentially leading, on the one hand, to the end of life as we know it on Planet Earth and, on the other, to unbounded opportunity to explore and co-create a new world. But unlike the explorers of old, we have the advantage of being able to draw both upon foreknowledge of the future and the wisdom of ages past. We live in what has been called the Information Age, when anyone with a connection to the internet has access to virtually all human knowledge. As we pass through the portal of 2012, we will graduate into the Age of Wisdom, when knowledge balanced by love becomes a powerful tool to propel humanity into a higher form of being. No longer will we misuse our gifts of knowledge for selfish purposes, like power and wealth for the few. In human history that is what destroyed civilizations. Rather we will join with collaborative partners in many realms in ventures that support the highest good of all.

Envision a New Way of Being

Just as you enroll in a course of study because you have an expectation of what you will gain from it—your desired outcome—to embark on the journey to 2012 and beyond you will benefit from beginning by going deep within and envisioning with Spirit the kind of world you would like to see on the other side of the Great Shift. Your vision of the new world and yourself in it is an important exercise to complete before considering how to manifest this vision. That doesn't mean there aren't going to be a few surprises—maybe lots of them—but your vision will give you something to hang on to whenever the turbulence increases.

Fifty years ago, my world history teacher asked our tenth grade class to jump one hundred years into the future and imagine a scene about how learning would take place in that world. I drew a picture of a person lying on a table, receiving direct communications into her consciousness through beams of light transmitted from a higher dimension. A couple of scientists in lab coats stood around observing and facilitating this process. My vision was featured on a local educational television program, and at fourteen I confidently explained to viewers that in the future we would be able to access knowledge telepathically. Now I don't think we're going to have to wait until 2057 to get there!

Many of you also have had dreams, visions, and insights into the future. While it's important that your vision be just that— yours—I'll share with you elements of mine to give you an idea of where I'm coming from, if you haven't figured that out by now! I've jotted down sentences that suggest some of the possibilities about the future we might co-create with Spirit and one another. As possibilities turn into probabilities and actual events, the vision allows for great flexibility and rearranging of parts and scenarios. More knowledge and wisdom will be revealed to us as we move toward and through 2012.

*****

Earth goes through a cleansing and purification which lifts off toxins and pollutants from the land, air, and seas and releases dark energy from a violent past, transmuting these into the highest light and creating a fresh start for all life and all that supports life on our planet.

Humanity and all beings in every realm recognize and celebrate their interconnectedness and hold the Unity Consciousness of Love and Light.

Human and other species on Planet Earth share her abundant resources, which she gives forth in due season. All have enough and live in harmony with her natural rhythms. Earth's natural resources are not depleted but are renewable.

Humanity has a cosmic consciousness and lives in harmony with the music of the spheres, a reflection of Divine Love and the natural laws of the Universe. Jesus' prayer, "on Earth as it is in Heaven," is fulfilled.

Beings of Light in other realms reveal themselves to us as friends and allies who support our new world and in turn seek our support in carrying forward their visions.

With all of Creation in harmonious balance, our Galaxy, the Milky Way, continues to expand and co-create new visions and new worlds. Old, outmoded systems end and return to stardust.

Life on Earth is joyous and creative, as each being receives abundant support in fulfilling its purpose and dreams and lives out its natural life in peace.

Lives of humans are much longer than before the Shift. Life spans of 120 or more years are common. Everyone sets an intention to be healthy and has a lifestyle that promotes health and wholeness of mind, body, and spirit. Disease and illness are unknown or temporary. Each person knows how to bring him-or herself back into balance if necessary. Healers in every community share the knowledge and wisdom of natural healing with children so that they may grow up experiencing the fullness of life.

Technology has advanced to support and extend human capacity. Advanced Artificial Intelligence is balanced with love, so that it may work in concert with humans, not in ways that are either subservient or overpowering to humans.

The education of children is overseen by their communities. Children are born telepathic and are advanced rapidly through basic subjects, completing the equivalent of an undergraduate degree by the time they are 12. Then they may pursue knowledge and experience in any subject in any way they choose: through virtual communities, mentoring programs on Earth and in other dimensions, travel, work experience, or other means not yet conceived.

All children born in the Galaxy are expected and greeted with joy by their communities. They are raised in loving homes with extended communal families. When they are old enough, they may travel anywhere on Earth or in the Galaxy to meet and learn from whatever groups they wish. Astral travel and teleportation are their most common means of travel.

The Earth's population of humans and animals is sustained by an abundance of natural resources. All have enough without hoarding food, water, and minerals. Communal gardens are found everywhere, and people enjoy planting, tending, and eating the fruit of the Earth as it comes into season. They harvest and preserve what remains and use it as needed.

Communication is primarily through telepathy between individuals or groups or through advanced personal microcomputers with instant access to all past knowledge and future possibilities in the Akashic Records. All beings are directly connected to Cosmic Intelligence and Love (God) so that there is no possibility of misunderstanding, and all knowledge is instantly available simultaneously for everyone.

Human communities are small, local groupings of people who choose to live together and who network with other communities nearby as well as across the Universe. Each person's gifts are valued and developed by the community for the highest good of the individual and the whole body. Creativity and self-expression, not conformity, are encouraged. Communities are governed by leaders chosen periodically, and all are trained for leadership and given opportunities to serve. Important decisions are made through group discernment in concert with the higher realms.

All communities are part of networks configured in a variety of ways to serve many purposes, such as communication among the dimensions and realms, distribution of resources to ensure that all have enough, co-creating new ideas and manifesting them, and facilitating intergalactic travel. No sense of separation exists within Unity Consciousness, but rather a recognition of and appreciation for individual and community differences and uniqueness. Cooperation and collaboration are the norms.

Many varieties of animals, sea creatures, plants, and minerals thrive on Earth, including new species unknown before the Great Shift. Communication between and among species is normal. Animals, like humans, consume only renewable foods and are not subject, while alive, to being eaten, abused, or neglected. They live out their natural lives and when dead may be consumed by other animals or humans.

Men and women are less gender distinctive. Their creative, kundalini energy is directed at giving birth to new creations of many kinds—art, music, literature, science, architecture, technology, food, species, and habitats as well as children. Earth's population is kept in balance naturally at a sustainable level.

*****

I could go on, but you've got the idea. You can spin out your own vision of the way life might be in the Universe and on Earth after the shift. All things are possible—as long as they balance knowledge with love and are wise and life-giving. If we're going to play in and with the higher realms, we'll have to look up and reach higher than we have before. It's time for our planet to take our place in the Universe as the home of wise, enlightened beings who live in harmony with the whole creation and serve the highest light. Otherwise, there's not going to be much to look forward to in the days ahead.

After creating your own vision of the kind of world you'd like to help give birth to, place yourself in it. Who are you? Where and how do you live? What are you doing in this world? Who are you connecting with? This makes your vision much more concrete and real. Draw or create your vision with art materials and revise as you feel guided. Creative visualization as a process is very helpful in realizing our dreams and visions. Because time is speeding up and will no longer govern us in the new world, our thoughts and visions will manifest in no time, so we will need to carefully construct what it is that we are trying to create. Be careful what you wish for! Ensure that whatever it is is in alignment with Spirit.

I've skipped over the transitional events and time it will take to get us to the point of living within the Unity Consciousness. Yet the seeds of much of what I've envisioned above are already in place. In the next chapters we'll look at these and other seeds we can help plant and nurture now so they'll flourish and flower when the time comes.

What is the knowledge we need now? How do we become the Wise Ones our Universe must be able to count on if our species and planet are to survive? Remember the message of the Hathors, that loving group consciousness from the Sirius star system channeled by Tom Kenyon, saying that human survival on Earth was not assured until the summer of 2007. That's too close for comfort. I don't know what shifted, but we must be doing something right. Lots of prayers, petitions, and actions are being taken by lots of people right now to support galactic efforts to help Earth release and rearrange what she needs to without blowing us off her face. And if there aren't enough possibilities of natural disasters, just reading the headlines reminds us of what a long way our species still has to go at this point. Our work is cut out for us.

CHAPTER FIVE: STRENGTHEN YOUR SPIRITUAL CONNECTION

As we prepare ourselves and our world for the Great Shift to Unity Consciousness, nothing is more important than our personal connections with Spirit. Drawing upon the spiritual wisdom available to us from many sources, ancient and current, focus on four essential elements of your spiritual preparation:

    1. Develop and explore your connection with Spirit;
    2. Expand your spiritual knowledge and practices;
    3. Do your inner work;
    4. Integrate and apply your knowledge and wisdom.

1. Develop and explore your connection with Spirit

Most people believe in a Higher Power or Supreme Presence, whether they call it God, Spirit, Allah, Source, Creative Intelligence, the Divine Mind, or something else. That's the place to start, with your connection to the God-presence. While you may also connect with angels and guides in other dimensions, begin with the highest, widest, deepest presence in the universe, which attracts us to itself and creates the oneness we all experience from time to time. Oneness is an awareness of Unity Consciousness. Seeing ourselves as expressions of the One does not diminish our individuality but reveals and strengthens our connectedness.

    Start with reflection on your concept of God or Spirit and how your sense of this presence grew within you. What was your earliest spiritual experience? Some of you may not feel you've had a personal experience of God, while for others it is common. Do you remember a numinous, mystical, direct experience of the

God-presence with which you resonated? What did it feel like? Where were you at the time? Were you able to share the experience with someone then? Have you had other such experiences? Do you *know* that this presence is real and always available to you or do you *believe* it because of your religious training or because others have told you about their experiences?

I wasn't aware of such an experience until I was an adult. I believed in God because I grew up in the church and because my family believed. I didn't *know* God until much later. I felt unseen presences when growing up and experienced synchronicities but didn't consider them divinely guided. When I was nine, my sixteen-year-old sister's death tested the family's faith. My father lost his for a time, my mother relied on hers, and I went numb inside. The numbness lasted for years. How many of us carry around unresolved grief, anger, and fear? It's time to process and release all of this. It's stuck energy, and it needs to flow again for us to get well and whole. Developing a strong connection with Source energy will enable us to release emotional, mental, physical, and spiritual blocks and stay centered in the high vibration of love.

Your relationship with Spirit is often colored by the religious tradition, if any, you grew up in. A great many people now consider themselves spiritual but not religious, having either no religious background or a less than satisfying one.

For those of you who either have left your religious traditions or are hanging on despite your concerns, I suggest that you spend some time recovering what you liked about your tradition, what nurtured you when you were growing up, what nourished your spirit. In my own case I loved singing in the choir, feeling my voice resonate with all the others in sacred music that uplifted my heart and soul, and I valued the senior minister in my home church and my youth group leaders. I appreciated their support, friendship, and wisdom. As a freshman in college I dated a Catholic boy and considered converting. My pastor wrote me a long letter and met with me while I was home for Easter break. He didn't try to keep me within the denomination I'd grown up in, but instead suggested joining another, more liturgical church that didn't require me to make the kind of permanent commitment required of Catholics. I took his advice and ending up staying within my tradition for a time, then dropping out for a couple of decades before coming back and rediscovering what I loved about being part of a faith community. I have been grateful for this man's wisdom ever since, just as I remain grateful for the opportunity I had to serve the church as a pastor, governing body leader, and consultant.

We must learn to see the positive in what we've experienced and not to throw the proverbial baby out with the bathwater. Religious institutions are only as good as the people within them. Your own high intentions and commitment can help others along their paths, if you choose to stay, and you may grow in humility and gratitude.

Whether or not you attend services or are part of a religious community is not what's most important. What matters is your own connection with the God-presence. That's what you need to cultivate, however you manage that. If you find a congregation that helps you develop and nurture that connection, so much the better. If not, look for a few like-minded people with whom you can share your spiritual journey. Help each other grow.

In my experience, a great many people in the west are attracted to spiritualities outside their own culture. Native American, Celtic, and eastern spiritualities, especially Buddhism, have been enormously popular with westerners in the past thirty years. I have been attracted to these spiritualities myself and have incorporated practices like meditation (quieting and expanding the mind) and mindfulness (staying in the present moment and observing life without judgment), among others, into my own spiritual practices. What appeals to each of us varies with our temperaments and what we are seeking. Rather than adopting the belief systems of whatever spiritual traditions they are attracted to, most people who explore them seem primarily interested in a transcendent experience of the divine presence, whether it's through a sweat lodge, group chant, or quiet meditation. We're all seeking transcendence, however we can find it. The hard part is bringing that back with us into our daily lives. Authentic mountaintop experiences are truly rare, and once we've had one we keep seeking more. Soon we will find the divine within us and will no longer need to seek outside what is readily available within.

Over the years I have studied and experienced mysticism across virtually all of the world's traditions in addition to the esoteric or hidden knowledge within my own Christian tradition. I have also studied in an ancient mystery school, The Ancient Mystical Order of the Rose Croix (AMORC), the Rosicrucian Order, which approaches the mystical from a scientific and philosophical perspective derived from a collection of manuscripts and teachings passed on from the most ancient of the mystery schools and wisdom traditions. I find many elements of all of these appealing and have learned a great deal from my deep and wide explorations. Yet I keep coming back to the knowledge and experience of the Christ as the pattern for what we are all evolving into. I find that I still have much to learn from observing and knowing the Jesus who brought the higher Christic consciousness to the planet, where he physically and spiritually anchored it. Rather than thinking of him in traditional Christian terms as the Savior or the Son of God who died for our sins, through direct experience with the Christ Consciousness I think of the Christ as the template for the transformation of humanity. We are all to become Christ-like in consciousness and capacity and to even go beyond what Jesus was able to do in his own short lifetime on Earth. What he taught the inner circle of his disciples, those who had ears to hear, including Mary Magdalene, his wife or close companion, was knowledge that is now available to all of us: the nature of the divine and of the universe, universal law, sacred geometry as the basic forms of matter, the power of love to raise and heal the human spirit, mind, and body, and more. This knowledge and wisdom is available to all through direct access to the mind and heart of God. This is the great news about the Great Shift!

We are already accessing this higher consciousness and catching glimpses of what awaits us. Now is the time to go deep within to find and amplify your own connection to God, Spirit, Source. Many of you regularly contact God in prayer. Prayer is needed, especially prayers of gratitude. What about prayers of petition? Ask for things you know or believe are part of divine will, such as for you to hold the high vibration of love, or for you to align with God's will, or for whatever outcome is for the highest good of all. We don't necessarily know what's in the mind of God, so we can't know that particular petitions we make are ultimately for the highest good. Free will is universal law. Particular outcomes exist as probabilities or possibilities. You must choose them if they are to be fulfilled, so choosing wisely is critical, especially if you're praying on someone else's behalf. Trust that spiritual guidance is available to help you work through whatever is for your or someone else's highest good.

If prayer is speaking to God, meditation is listening. Years ago I learned the techniques of Centering Prayer through the work of Father Thomas Keating, a Cistercian monk. Similar to eastern meditation, it involves quieting the "monkey mind" filled with impulses, fragments of thoughts, mental lists–chatter from all kinds of sources. The purpose of Centering Prayer is to allow an inner stillness to grow and connect you with Source energy. You are then to hold this stillness as long as possible or desirable, basking in the spiritual connection and listening for the whisperings of Spirit. Emptying or focusing the mind is part of most eastern meditation, which allows the individual self to become less in order to merge into Universal Oneness.

Everyone is different and drawn to practices reflecting his or her personality and understanding. The point is to develop and strengthen your own capacity to connect and communicate in some form with Spirit. Practice this daily until it becomes second nature, even though it's really first nature—our most basic expression of who we are—an aspect of the One.

2. Expand your spiritual knowledge and practices

A good place to begin an intentional expansion of spiritual knowledge and practices is to examine and reflect on your own life. The art and practice of reflection is essential to our spiritual growth. Excavating our lives for their meaning, for the key life lessons we have learned, is a way of illuminating our spiritual paths with all of their twists and turns through the labyrinth of life.

One way to begin your reflection is to make a timeline. Draw a straight line across a page with the left end representing your birth and the right end representing where you are now. Then mark the points of the three highest highs and three lowest lows of your life on this time line. Next, spend a few quiet moments asking yourself if you felt the presence of God in those moments or if you had any awareness of spiritual presence at the best and/or worst times of your life. Whether you have a religious background or not, you will have had personal experiences which defined who you are and your relationship with Spirit.

As we prepare for our journey through 2012, we'll need to be able to clearly sense, feel, or experience in some way the gift of spiritual presence. If you don't now, I encourage you to begin a daily practice of prayer or meditation and journaling to explore and express your own spiritual connection–past, present, and future.

Journaling is another great way to reveal and record your spiritual journey. Begin to journal daily or at least a couple of times a week what's going on in your life, how you are feeling, what you're thinking, and where Spirit is in all of this. Ask Spirit for insights, intuition, dreams, and experiences that will make you more and more aware of your spiritual connection with God and God's creation. As you become more intentional and disciplined about finding and strengthening your spiritual connection , you will develop the ability to shift your consciousness there instantly when you need guidance or find yourself in the midst of chaos and need to regain a calm, peaceful, loving center.

Tom Kenyon and his partner, Judy Sion, have advised people through the messages of the Hathors to work with the image of a holon. You visually construct a holon as two tetrahedrons or four-sided pyramids (three sides rising to a peak and a bottom—one of the five Platonic solids from which all sacred geometry that drives physical form derives) with their bottoms touching, one pointed toward the heavens, one toward the Earth. This holon becomes a diamond shape with you in the center sitting or lying on the flat middle surface, completely enclosed in this etheric shape. Envision it constructed of golden white light that comes down from the center of the galaxy into the pyramid pointing upward and continues down into the center of the Earth through the pyramid pointing downward. See yourself safe and secure and held in Divine Love within that space, and it will hold you stable in the midst of chaos. Work on imagining that holon in your mind's eye. Be able to go there in the blink of an eye when the time comes. It's a perfect place to go when you're feeling the least bit unsettled about anything, especially in the physical world around you. Being able to create and hold the energy of the holon will give you a sense of security and empowerment. Try it often.

You may have developed other practices that enable you to feel connected with Spirit. Sharing intentionally high group energy is one I particularly enjoy. When I am with others who are praying, chanting, singing, meditating, dancing, healing, or otherwise connecting with each other and with Spirit, the energy can get very high very fast. Who needs alcohol or drugs? We get natural highs by opening and joining our minds, hearts, and hands.

Find or create a group to support you as you prepare for the Great Shift. While a local group is desirable, through phone and email you can create a group anywhere. Many virtual groups have formed online under the guidance of a spiritual leader. If you join one of these web-based sites, use your discernment skills to ensure that the group is supportive, spiritually aligned, and focused on the highest good of all. Choose your virtual community wisely.

In addition to reflecting on your spiritual path and developing basic daily practices, study and expand your knowledge through reading, workshops, and research. So much material is currently available and so many gifted and experienced teachers are teaching that you won't have difficulty finding sources to lead you down the trails of the interests you develop. The list of resources in Appendix B is a place to start. As adults, you are self-guided learners, responsible for your own education and offered such a wide range of choices that you will have to exercise discretion and discernment to choose what is best suited for you at any step along the path. Oprah Winfrey's recent TV and online class with spiritual teacher Eckhart Tolle was a fascinating new way to offer assistance with basic spiritual development to the widest possible audiences. We will see more of these technology-assisted interactive spiritual study opportunities as people seek them out. Exploring and expanding consciousness through study, especially within a community, can be very exciting and stimulating. Be open to new concepts and perspectives as you advance along the spiraling path toward wisdom and truth.

3. Do your inner work

Connecting with Spirit, releasing what no longer serves you and attracting to yourself what will support and enrich your life and illuminate your purpose is your inner work. This is a process that takes time and effort. A lifetime of old stuck energy and patterns of thinking and behaving will be released, if you work at it and allow it to happen. Spiritual energy healing can be extremely helpful in the process. This high level work with people's energy fields can assist shifting and releasing quickly when someone is ready to give up ingrained patterns or behaviors which are self-destructive or harmful to others.

For example, one very common pattern is the victim mentality. People who see themselves as victims feel powerless and resist taking responsibility for their decisions and actions. If things go wrong, it's someone else's fault. Blaming others is an energetic pattern that needs to be released to free them to move on in their lives. At some point they may indeed have been victimized and since then have not been able to step into their own power. Being mature spiritually means recognizing how your own choices led to who you are now. The recognition of our God-given free will is essential to break this pattern. If you make a choice you wish you hadn't, learn from it. Reflect on it and write about in your journal and ask Spirit to assist you in not repeating it. Then just release it. Don't keep blaming yourself or feeling guilty—that's as negative and harmful to you as blaming someone else for a choice you made. Self-forgiveness is an essential part of inner work. So is forgiving others and seeing situations that hurt you or made you angry from their perspectives. Often people are not aware of how what they say and do affects others. You can gently help them understand that, but you can't do their work for them. Your own work is enough. And while you're doing it, be compassionate and gentle with yourself as well as others. We're all slow learners sometimes!

Believe it or not, we chose what lessons we needed to learn before we came into this life, just as we chose our families and friends for what we could learn from and offer to each other. To graduate this time around from the school of life we need to become loving, forgiving, generous, grateful people serving the highest light and assisting others on their paths to the higher dimensions. That's the desired learning outcome leading to the Great Shift to Unity Consciousness!

If you're finding that patterns in your life with undesirable outcomes keep repeating, pay attention now. Find a spiritual counselor or energy healer to help you discern what's going on and what you can do to shift the pattern, release blocked energy and move forward on your path. A decade ago, Carolyn Myss, a healer and teacher who's published some very helpful material, wrote *Why People Don't Heal and How They Can.* The main point is that sometimes people are afraid to give up their worn-out patterns of behavior or illnesses because in a perverse way they get benefits from them: more attention and sympathy, the comfort of the familiar, letting others be responsible for them and their wellness, being afraid of being in control, and so on. Often they don't even recognize they're holding on to these patterns that no longer serve them. Until they confront their own choices and do their own inner work, they won't get well, even if they continue to visit doctors and healers, who they will then blame for not "fixing" them. Don't ever take responsibility for fixing anyone except yourself, and only then with spiritual assistance!

As 2012 approaches, we're all going to have to step up the pace of self-healing and assisting others who are ready to heal. That's essential if we're going to be ready for the new world awaiting us on the other side of the shift. One approach that in recent years has proved helpful to many is found in the Abraham-Hicks material, especially the book *Ask and It is Given: Learning to Manifest Your Desires.* Abraham is a higher dimension group consciousness channeled by Esther Hicks. She and her husband, Jerry, have built a substantial business around the Abraham teachings, which are highly repetitive and center on the Law of Attraction: attracting from the Universe what you desire and not attracting what you don't. Although oversimplified, the popular spiritual movie *The Secret*, in which the Hickses had a hand, included much of the same material on the Law of Attraction. Like attracts like expresses it in a nutshell. If you want to attract high vibration energy and participate in the transformation to Unity Consciousness, you'll have to hold a high vibration yourself. A very useful page of the *Ask and It is Given* book is the one that lists 22 emotions from low to high. At the bottom, the lowest vibration emotions are fear and depression. At the top are love, empowerment, and joy. Only the top seven on the list are what we might consider positive. Number seven is contentment, number eight boredom. Yet boredom can lead us to examine our lives and find something to which to attach our dreams, visions, and passions.

Mostly we find ourselves somewhere in between the highs and the lows. If you aren't sure what you're feeling at any given moment, it's worth getting the book for that list in order to test daily what and how you are feeling. Your feelings are the best gauge of what vibration you're holding at any given moment. That's why it's so important to try to get into and stay at the vibration of love, particularly when faced with difficult situations.

The Abraham material also teaches people how to move up the emotional ladder, one rung at a time, through intention and will. That's important inner work. It helps people know that they to a large extent can choose and control how they feel, and that's empowering, especially to those prone to depression, who often feel powerless to change.

Our inner work is largely emotional, mental, and spiritual but helps on the physical level, too. Illness, dis-ease, manifests in the physical body (unless it's genetic) after it has manifested in the energetic fields around the body that hold our emotional and mental patterns. So inner work and energy healing are preventive and would save billions of dollars spent on health care every year if people used these natural processes to restore wellness and whole-ness. Technology is also entering energy work. A healer friend has a computerized system that helps people break ancestral patterns and bring the body into balance through sophisticated programs and natural substances. After the shift this kind of work will be mainstream, rather than sidelined by the health care industry and government regulators.

4. Integrate and apply your knowledge

To complete our basic spiritual preparation for 2012 and beyond, we must integrate and apply what we've learned. As we move into an age that will emphasize unity rather than separation, we need practice in applying our new spiritual knowledge so that it becomes wisdom. Wisdom is, after all, the integration and tempering of knowledge with experience. Experience is the test of knowledge, and knowledge guides the experience.

Wisdom is also characterized by intention. The Wise Ones among the ancients were those who brought spiritual understanding to their tribes and communities for everyone's highest good. That is a standard by which each of us can measure what we're passing on to others: does it benefit all life now and in the future? Life after the shift is going to be about cooperation, not competition, and that will mean quite a shift for those of us who live in consumer cultures. If we hope not merely to survive but thrive, we will need to be concerned even about the insects in our ecosystems and their integral part in the vast, interconnected web of creation. Seeing the connections is knowledge and understanding the creative intelligence behind them is wisdom. If we are not awestruck by the natural world or grateful for all that is, we're not yet ready for the shift.

Our practical work, applying what we know through experience to transform it into wisdom, begins with clarifying what we hope to do for what purpose and naming the desired outcome. Setting an intention for the highest good of all is essential before we take any action. Intention directs our thoughts and energy. When I teach or offer spiritual energy healing with Arcing Light, I begin by stating my intention. It always involves being an open, clear, loving channel of Divine healing love and light for the highest good for all concerned. This helps me to stay spiritually aligned. The work of healing is the individual's in concert with Spirit. I am simply a tool or instrument to help bring about what both desire. My job is not to fix but to allow and assist. That's always good to remember when we do spiritually guided work in the world. Hopefully, all of our work is spiritually guided, or at least we may choose that as our intention.

Gratitude is a good measure of spiritual maturity. Being grateful for everything in your life, even what you considered at the time negative or hurtful, helps you to see the lessons the experience allowed you to learn and the good that came out of it. "Light shines in the darkness, and the darkness does not overcome it," a verse from the Gospel of John, reminds us to trust in the wisdom and love of God who sees all from the highest and widest perspective, while we glimpse only a fragment. To measure your own sense of gratitude, try reflecting on how you grew from experiences and circumstances you considered at first to be devastating. To give thanks in all things is to release the power of the negative to harm or block you on your spiritual path. This teaching is one we'll need to master as we move through 2012 and beyond.

Humility is another spiritual gift that takes us closer to the Great Shift to Unity Consciousness. A finely developed sense of humility helps us keep our egos in check and our accomplishments in perspective. The news is filled with stories of those who misuse power and money out of ego and greed. What they have in common is the loss of any sense of humility. People deferred to them and allowed them to reach unrealistic heights, only to fall harder and farther when they got out of balance and became little gods in their own settings. Some have managed to redeem themselves with the help of Spirit. They've had to develop a healthy sense of humility, to recognize where they'd gone wrong and take responsibility for their missteps. Whether as individuals or nations, good intentions alone are not enough. We must stay aligned with our intentions through our actions. With the Great Shift on the way, we don't have time to make such serious errors anymore.

We learn wisdom through experiences that reveal to us where we missed the mark. That's the definition of the word "sin," by the way, a word I intentionally don't use any more because it feels judgmental and guilt-filled. In Greek "sin" means missing the mark. We all do that on occasion, and it's a whole lot easier to admit that than to call ourselves "sinners." We're not sinners. We're people who have a lot to learn and need help from Spirit to get that.

As we learn to master our selves, to hold the ego in check or pump it up a bit when necessary, always testing our feelings and decisions through our constant communication with Spirit, as we commit to following our guidance and developing our spiritual gifts so that we may serve a higher purpose than material or personal success, we become the wise ones we have been seeking. Who first said, "We are the ones we have been waiting for"? It's been attributed to a lot of people lately because it's being said a lot. We are stepping into our roles as wise leaders and helping others step into theirs. We no longer need to look outside ourselves for answers. We find them within. The kin-dom of God is within you.

When you are spiritually aligned and following your inner wisdom, you will find many opportunities to serve a higher purpose. One striking example of this happened as a group of spiritual energy healers I was traveling with was seated on an Egypt Air flight heading home from Cairo. We'd been there to anchor high vibration energy around the pyramids on the Giza Plateau and in and around the ancient temples at Luxor. We'd had some amazing experiences and had just settled in for a long flight to New York when we heard shouting a few rows ahead of us. An American woman and an Egyptian Muslim man were arguing about their seats. The woman called the man a "male chauvinist pig" and the alarm bells went off. Here we were on the ground in Egypt, on an Egyptian plane in a Muslim country where women were veiled and did not argue with men, who considered themselves their superiors. Our group spontaneously began to surround the situation with loving energy and asked for spiritual assistance. Things were getting ugly as passengers on both sides of the argument shouted at each other, and security police rushed in. At the very least our departure could have been delayed, causing some of us to miss our connections. At worst it could have precipitated violence or an international incident. We kept holding the high vibration energy with the intention of a peaceful outcome. In a matter of minutes, things calmed down for no apparent reason. The man, smiling, came over to the woman and offered her his seat. She apologized to him, the flight attendants got everyone seated, the police left, and we all breathed a sign of relief. Right on time, our flight lifted off for New York. We knew that spiritual energy healing had made the difference.

Anyone can do the same in a situation that threatens to explode. Just set your intention and breathe love and light into the situation. It can work in all kinds of settings. The power of your positive intention helps bring people into alignment with the higher vibration energy, especially when it's held by a group, and releases fear, anger, and tension. This situation and its favorable outcome convinced us that people working together for a common, higher purpose can bring about the change the world needs. Remember the morphic resonance or energy fields of Unity Consciousness we talked about earlier and the critical mass of people it will take to bring about the Great Shift? Every act that resolves peacefully and for everyone's highest good improves the chances that the shift will happen soon, and we will no longer see ourselves as separated by race, gender, nationality or religion but as aspects of the One God, Source Energy, united in love at ever more complex levels of being. It is truly remarkable how much we can accomplish together. Our group on the plane felt empowered and affirmed.

Trusting that we can find the answers we seek and create the opportunities and support systems we desire, life on the path through 2012 becomes less frightening and more appealing. We have much to look forward to, and that's what we want to keep in mind as we continue our preparation for the Great Shift.

CHAPTER SIX: CHOOSE YOUR LOCATION AND LIFESTYLE

Emergencies and Physical Changes of Lifestyle

A headline caught my eye recently as it scrolled across my computer screen. It was about a small town in northern Michigan locked in controversy over whether a company would be allowed to build a $79 million center there which would create hundreds of jobs. I wondered what kind of a company would not be welcomed by a community suffering from recession—a toxic chemical plant? A munitions factory? A camp to train terrorists? The company in question turned out to be a survival preparedness firm that equips and trains people across the U.S. to survive disasters of all kinds! It designs customized survival plans right down to temporary housing, water and food, medical supplies, even GPS tracking, all aimed at keeping its customers alive up to two weeks following a crisis. The premium plan even includes flying in supplies or evacuating clients, if necessary and possible. And why did some in the town want to keep out this company? Because it apparently caters to high-end clients. The idea that those with money would survive while the rest would not was too much for an opposition group, while the town fought for the business. This story tells you something about what people are thinking: there's profit in disaster, people need to prepare for natural and human-caused catastrophes, and nobody wants to be left behind. Shades of the old bomb and fall-out shelters of my youth!

Intrigued, I went to this company's website to check it out. Sure enough, the all-male company execs were offering customized "Family Response Plans" and access to a 24/7 Operations

Center—the one to be built in Michigan—for "members." What the tariff was wasn't disclosed. The site encouraged visitors to read news headlines on display from around the world to raise their awareness about the kinds of incidents that could disrupt their lives: "Bacteria race ahead of drugs, "one headline read, while others alerted the potential customer to climate extremes or terrorist acts.

Another page on the site pointed out lack of awareness on the public's part and lack of preparedness on the part of government agencies at all levels should various kinds of disasters occur. The company's CEO pointed out that Americans spend over $500 billion each year on insurance to protect their material possessions and very little on protecting themselves from the unforeseen. True enough, I thought. What an interesting perspective! Raising people's awareness that they have even more to fear than they thought would certainly lead some to make the decision to get ready.

As you've already seen, I'm a big advocate of preparedness, but not of fear. My concern here is with the fear-based approach to what may come rather than the entrepreneurial goals of this company. They claim to offer disaster plans for as little as $500, an affordable figure for most Americans, even though you could get much of the same information from the internet or from a growing number of books like a few I bought, listed in Appendix B: *When Technology Fails: A Manual for Self-Reliance and Planetary Survival, Peak Oil Prep: Prepare for Peak Oil, Climate Change and Economic Collapse* (this looked liked a bargain since it covered a lot of bases!), and *Gardening When It Counts: Growing Food in Hard Times.* Still, I could see why busy people might want to pay survival experts a substantial sum to set them up, as opposed to getting ready on their own. But if they did that, they'd miss the opportunity to reflect on what kind of world they want to survive in and to co-create that world with Spirit and a community of their choice. Survival in 3D without Unity Consciousness in a higher and wider dimension is not particularly desirable, if you consider the kind of existence people motivated by fear are likely to create.

We've all seen or heard of futuristic stories where survivors of catastrophes stalk the land, fighting off marauders, thieves, and murderers with guns, knives, and their wits. In fact, the world has already seen many such scenarios. Did you notice any looters in New Orleans after Katrina hit? Where lawlessness reins, good citizens are no match for armed gangs and desperate hunters and hoarders of food, water, and money—not that money will mean much in some of the scenarios we examined earlier. Who would want to survive in such a world? "Beam me up, Scotty," is all I can say. Without fear of what lies beyond death, I would rather be lifted off into another dimension, another planet, or to wherever heaven is than stay behind in such a world. I don't know what the survival prep firm thinks will happen to their clients after their two weeks of support are up, but I'm betting they'll be in for a rude shock. Maybe that's when members' guns, grenades, and other self-defense equipment will be airlifted in as the pilot waves goodbye.

If this is not the future you envision, what will yours look like instead? What kind of physical preparations for life on a different kind of Earth should we be thinking about now? That, of course, depends on which of the five scenarios in Chapter Three you believe is most likely or are working to co-create. It also depends entirely on your own spiritual preparation, covered in the last chapter. Let's face it–that's the only kind that matters if Scenario One, extreme destruction, takes place, as we won't be around long enough to worry about what happens afterwards. But if one of the other scenarios is what you're hoping for or expecting, then a whole host of physical preparations might be considered.

One kind of situation you may face is an event for which you are forewarned, like a hurricane, tornado or tsunami—if your community has a good warning system. This year surprising winter tornados in Arkansas, Tennessee, and Kentucky claimed 56 lives and caused billions in damages, yet supposedly 100% of the communities were forewarned through their emergency network systems. Are people paying attention or not believing that anything will happen to them?

During the '90's my husband and I lived in a hurricane-prone area, a barrier island off the east coast. Residents knew they'd have several days warning before they'd have to evacuate, and a great many of them would wait until the last minute, then scramble to round up what would fit in their cars along with themselves and their pets. Late evacuees would get stuck in heavy traffic on the island's one road to the mainland without having a plan in mind as to where they might go, which direction would result in less traffic, and how to stay out of the path of the hurricane.

One summer while in seminary I served as an intern in a church that had been entirely rebuilt after a local hurricane wiped out its predecessor, along with many of the members' homes. As I visited and talked with members over those weeks, about three years after the event, the number one topic still remained the impact of the hurricane on their lives. They told me their stories and what they'd lost and what they wished they'd saved. Do you know what the most regrettable loss was to most of them? Their family pictures—the photos of themselves and loved ones at various stages of their lives. It was as though their pasts and memories had been wiped out with the disappearance of those photos. Yet how many people are thinking about grabbing their photo albums as they head out the door—unless they've spent some time thinking about what they would take in case of an emergency?

That's why it's helpful to think ahead about what is most important and meaningful in your lives that will sustain you through a time of loss. Yes, you'll need food, water, clothing, meds, pet supplies, bedding, tax records, licenses, wills, and other important papers., but what about your wedding pictures or the locket that was your grandmother's or the first love letter given you by your spouse? Things of the heart are harder to replace than stuff, especially if the stuff is insured. Any kind of disaster or likely incident for which you are forewarned should include some representative items of family or personal history with sentimental value. Include something for each family member, even if you only have room for one or two small items. People cling to those kinds of things through a great loss.

Where will you go if your home is destroyed or uninhabitable? Think about that, however unpleasant doing so may be. I'm talking about possibilities beyond temporary housing, like FEMA trailers or moving in with your brother-in-law. What if climate change or a human-caused event wipes out your town or your region? Where could you go and how would you get there? Who would go with you? As you think about these things, you may trigger emotions such as fear, anger, anxiety, or grief. Those are natural. Observe them, then surround them with the pure white light of love and allow them to be released. People who've experienced traumatic events often carry long afterwards the marks of the trauma. That's what Post-Traumatic Stress Disorder (PTSD), common among soldiers and other trauma survivors, is about. Any kind of anxiety-causing situation recreates the feelings of the earlier one, in which helplessness, fear, and other lower vibration emotions were experienced. If you can gently allow them to surface long enough to transmute them to the love energy, you may be able to release them completely or at least in stages. Rather than create new fears and anxieties about the coming changes, I hope to give you a new sense of control and expectation, while offering options and guidance for the best outcomes.

On the one hand, we don't want to imagine something undesirable into existence by making it too vivid or realistic, like a horror movie, a genre I've never found the least bit appealing. I was sixteen when I saw Alfred Hitchcock's "Psycho" when it first came out. I have never been as freaked out by anything in my life! For decades afterwards I was leery of taking showers alone in the house. A vivid imagination can be both a blessing and a curse. We don't want to dwell on the worst and help manifest it. That's crossing the line. On the other hand, ignoring the possibilities doesn't help either. What we can do is imagine the consequences of certain events or situations realistically without getting emotionally upset by various possible outcomes. Here's where training in Centering Prayer or meditation that quiets the mind or allows thoughts to float by without attaching to them emotionally comes in handy. I've found that I can consider all of the possible disasters I listed early on in this book along with the level of loss of life and property that might flow from them without fear. What allows me to do that is being able to look at them from a higher perspective, one that sees that all of life will continue in one way or another after the event we call death, and that all is in divine order and has a purpose we cannot necessarily see. My attitude is based on trust and knowing through experience that I am a part of the oneness of creation and that my essence will be preserved no matter what. That being the case, I don't mind transitioning at the appropriate time to my next experience. I just don't want to go out with fear in my heart rather than love.

If the energy you put into imagining a likely future is held at a high vibration, then that is more likely to be the way you experience whatever happens. You may have to compensate for a whole lot of other people's fear, so practice staying in the heart in all things. I admire the orchestra that played "Nearer My God to Thee" as the Titanic sank. That took faith. It also took their minds off what was happening. An essential part of your preparation for a possible disaster is looking at what might happen without going into fear.

That's a part of any disaster preparedness training conducted by organizations like FEMA, the Red Cross, the Humane Society of the US, military, police, firefighter, and EMT training, among others. I took DART (Disaster Animal Response Team) training through the Humane Society about fifteen years ago. We were trained in the field as well as in the classroom and learned how to do everything from bandage a frightened dog and trap a skittish cat to hauling a horse out of a ditch it couldn't climb out of itself. I was amazed at the skills and no-nonsense approach of our teachers. You expect vets to know that kind of thing, but the people who taught me weren't squeamish in the least. I don't much like the sight of blood and can't watch having my own drawn, so I found the women who trained the DART group I was in heroic. In emergency situations your heart still hurts for the people and the animals. You just learn to get past the fear. In fact, compassion for victims of disasters opens people's hearts and is part of what will lift the planet to the higher vibration of love.

I highly recommend that everyone take some kind of emergency training with a local agency, including first aid and CPR. Being able to take action in a variety of situations you may encounter, even in your home or on a trip, makes you feel more confident and useful. Trust me, your skills will be needed in the future, one way or another, so look into what is being offered in your community or create your own program. Disaster preparedness classes are offered over the internet now, too, so no excuses, okay? We need people who can think and act clearly in emergencies. At the very least, don't be one of those who stands around watching others save lives. You can always hold love energy around any situation, just as described earlier on the Egypt Air flight.

The Possibility of Migration

Returning to the earlier question, where would you go if you couldn't go back to your home for months, years, or maybe ever? We're hearing from many sources that migration may be in our futures. Can you foresee conditions in which that would be necessary? One is lack of water in your area. Living in New Mexico for several years made me aware of how difficult water can be to come by. On our ranch north of Santa Fe we had to drill down nearly 1000 feet to hit water and even then the quality was so poor that not even a double reverse osmosis system could rid it of a foul taste and smell. My guidance told me that living in that drought-prone area was not to be a part of our family's future. Our ranch was full of pottery shards and other evidence of the Gallina people—the country cousins of the Anasazi—who had lived on our land centuries earlier. When prolonged, severe drought hit the area in the eleventh and twelfth centuries, roaming bands killed off those whose land was still fertile, and the great center of Anasazi culture, Chaco Canyon, was abandoned, along with the civilization it had spawned all the way from Mexico to Colorado. Eventually, what remained of those early people settled in the Rio Grande Valley, where water was available, and became the pueblo Indians whose villages and reservations still populate this arid land. We can't assume that we will be immune to such conditions, even with our high tech culture.

You expect drought in the southwest—at least if you pay attention. Yet a recent issue of *National Geographic* contained a story about how water parks, entertainment centers, and golf courses are spreading everywhere in the southwest, especially in Arizona and Nevada. Does this make any sense at all? No. Does that stop people from doing it and making vast sums of money off of developing the desert? No. Does that prevent thousands every year from moving into these water-poor states and consuming this precious resource to the point of water wars as a part of their future? No, but it should. And this is in a country that should know better. Sub-Saharan Africa is another matter, where mass migration to survive famine and drought are well known. We are setting up conditions in what is now a first-world country that will result in mass migration out of drought-stricken areas. Remember *Grapes of Wrath* and the dust-bowl of the 1930's across the mid-section of the country? Watch the film version of Steinbeck's novel sometime which shows once-rich cropland turned to dust blowing in the wind. Is this a part of our future?

Reports in my local paper show that the drought in North Carolina is likely to last at least through the scorching summer again. Since the region's municipalities never expected to be down to their last 30-180 days of water, it's time for drastic measures. As long as the public and businesses are allowed to consume at their normal rates, we will face severe restrictions in the coming months. My husband is thinking seriously about planting drought-resistant grasses and plants usually found in the western U.S. in place of the nearly dead fescue grass that was our front lawn. This is our own personal experience of climate change.

Will we be driven out of our home by drought and wild fires? We thought we were being smart by not owning real estate in hurricane- and drought–prone zones, yet ended up in a place where we never expected to experience weather extremes. What have you been observing in your region? As you get to know your local ecosystem and its watershed, observe the weather patterns and note anomalies. These are the signs of the times and give us clues and advance warning on what might be coming. Not long ago *USA Today* ran a map called "Disaster Declarations" by county throughout the U.S., showing which had been included in federal disaster declarations up to 13 times in the past ten years. Those with the most disasters, not surprisingly, were along the coasts, especially the Gulf Coast, but Southern California, the Pacific North West, North Dakota, Oklahoma, the New England states, and a corridor through Tennessee, Kentucky, West Virginia and Ohio had a considerable number. Those with none or few disasters included western Wyoming, parts of Nevada and Utah and northern Michigan. Come to think of it, maybe the survival company mentioned had figured this out when they chose "Up North," as we say in Michigan. The western states mentioned just haven't experienced their greatest risks yet—drought and earthquakes—although wildfires abound.

Is there any place that won't be vulnerable to Earth changes and human-caused catastrophes? Not really, but some are more vulnerable than others, so ask your guidance where you need to be. A friend of mine says she expects to be guided at the appropriate time, even if it's just to be out of town while something is going on in her area. A number of people I know, including myself, have been guided to move in the past five years, so pay attention to your intuition and to what's going on around you and around the world.

If a pole shift should occur, regions that are now considered mostly uninhabitable could be safer than heavily populated regions. Can you see yourself migrating to Greenland or the Yukon Territory? Visualize it without fear. Presumably it would be more temperate in the far north after a pole shift, but there's something about making a trek like that and setting up a yurt on a glacier that boggles the mind. Most of us will just stay put and make do, whatever that looks like.

Many, however, will have to migrate as the Earth heats up and the electromagnetic patterns weaken and shift. If your home is no longer habitable, then you'll have to find a new one. Thousands who migrated out of Louisiana and Mississippi after Katrina found good, even better situations for themselves in other locations. Migration will happen because of economic and geopolitical shifts as well. As the Industrial Revolution took hold in this country, jobs migrated to manufacturing facilities, like the auto plants in Detroit, and so did the people. Now Michigan is adapting to an economy where the Big Three automakers are no longer dominant, and jobs are migrating elsewhere. How many places have lost hundreds and thousands of jobs to low wage economies abroad? When you call customer service these days do you talk with someone in the Philippines or India?

Get used to the idea of migration, whatever the reason. It may very well be a part of your future and not because it's your first choice. More and more it will become a matter of survival and not only temporarily. Just as birds and animals migrate to food and water sources, so may we. In the future it's possible that national boundaries will no longer be barriers to migration. This may come about as a matter of necessity.

Overpopulation is a huge problem on Earth. We're at 6.67 billion people and counting. Check out the world population clock at the U.S. Census Bureau's website (www.census.gov/main/www/popclock.html) to see just how quickly humans are overrunning the planet. Natural disasters also contribute to shortages of grains on which most of the world's people depend, and not even migration will solve the problem of growing famine. The World Bank recently announced that food prices worldwide have increased 83% in the past three years! Already 20 million children are estimated to be starving. As we destroy rainforests and old growth forests, pollute our water sources with toxins, and use up the world's grain to feed animals we kill to eat and for ethanol to run our cars, it doesn't take a rocket scientist to see that we're heading toward a time of great peril. Add to that the fact that we may already have reached peak oil—the point at which the world's production of oil begins its terminal decline—and we have the makings of global economic recession and war over resources unless we get our collective act together very soon. Nature's way of thinning out populations is pandemics, and man's way is war. However it happens, the world can't sustain all of us in the future. Spiritual guides tell us that there are already twenty times more people than Mother Earth's carrying capacity can comfortably support. So let's talk about reducing consumption as part of our preparation for life in the future on Planet Earth.

Presently the U.S. alone, with less than five percent of the world's population, consumes nearly 25% of Earth's resources. That means we're taking more than five times our fair share. This pattern is now being emulated by developing countries with vastly greater populations, like China and India, where people want the same comforts and luxuries western industrialized nations have enjoyed for the past half century. What does this add up to? More and more scarcity. Add to that industrial-sized waste with nowhere to go except into the Earth and her oceans. These demographics factor into the 2012 scenarios presented earlier. If we are to survive and thrive on our planet, we need to change our patterns of consumption. Remember the old mantra of the early environmental movement—reduce, reuse, recycle? This advice needs to be adopted by every person, every business, and every nation on Earth right now. It is a key part of the Great Shift in mass consciousness. Unless people get that we must collaborate on strategies to ensure that all have enough, all won't. And that doesn't mean just in the third world. Shortages will exist everywhere, and if fear prevails over love, we've had it.

Adapting Your Lifestyle to Changing Conditions

Everyone's physical preparation for the shift would benefit greatly from creating and adapting to a simpler lifestyle that uses fewer resources and relies more on collaborative and communal efforts to meet basic needs. For years I studied and taught about the simplicity movement, summed up in the statement "Live simply, so others can simply live." I described simplicity in my last book, *Graceful Living: Your Faith, Values, and Money in Changing Times*, as one of seven graceful living concepts or spiritual attitudes and practices. I said then that simplicity is generally characterized by "a desire to redefine the good life as one close to nature, to family and friends, to community and to God. Simplicity is about shedding things that don't bring deep satisfaction and an inner sense of peace and well being." I went on to say that not everything considered part of the simplicity movement seems simple, like growing your own food, making your own clothes, possibly home-schooling your children, getting along with one car instead of two, using public transportation, or taking a lower-paying job that reduces stress and allows for more time with family and community activities. "There are trade-offs in any lifestyle choice," I said, "and simple living is about defining and choosing what those trade-offs will be."

Choosing a simpler lifestyle is a good example of where our spiritual preparation overlaps physical preparation. Learning to get along with less creates more for others. That's a justice issue, allowing for all to have enough, including other species, and a sustainability issue for the Earth—to reduce our use of scarce resources and the piling up of waste.

Here's an exercise for you. Spend a few days imagining everything you own or use that you could get along without. Consider also what you would do with the stuff you don't really need. Could someone else make use of it rather than sending it to the landfill? Could some of it be sold to pay off debt or given away to charities? What would you have left? Could you fit it all in one room in your home? Three rooms? If so, could you live in a smaller home that would cost less and use less energy to heat and cool? This is very counter cultural. Americans in particular are used to larger spaces and the accumulation of more and more stuff to fill them. What would the trade-offs be if you reduced your living quarters and their contents down to what you really needed that would still allow you to be comfortable? I grew up in a three-bedroom one-bath home that accommodated a five-person household. Now, two of us live in twice that amount of space filled with our stuff. Yet millions in what is the world's wealthiest country live in poverty. The inequity is painful to contemplate, yet difficult to change. As we go through 2012 and the Great Shift, all of us will be required to reset our priorities and share the Earth's abundance. In the final analysis, if we can build our contentment on the foundation of divine love and relationship with all that exists, we will be sure to always have enough.

On the physical plane we can co-create with Spirit new ways of living after the Great Shift. Instead of living in isolation from others, each having a household full of stuff, we'll likely be living in communities. Communal living allows us to share what we have so that we all don't need duplicates of the basics. We'll go over that in some detail in Chapter Eight, on creating your community. For now, consider mentally stripping down your lifestyle to the bare essentials and make a list of what these would be. Refer to it often and revise your list, paring it down even more, if you can. Find a place to gather and store emergency equipment to which you can add other essentials if you need to leave home in a hurry for an indefinite period of time.

My cousin Carl, a retired engineer and Air Force Colonel, is someone whose brain I'm picking as I prepare for the physical changes likely to be part of our future. Maybe you know someone like him. Carl is a real outdoors man, a hiker, camper, and hunter well trained in wilderness survival. Last summer he spent two weeks alone on Isle Royale, a remote national park in Lake Superior off Michigan's Upper Peninsula. Carl spent the better part of a year thinking about, gathering, and making his gear for the trip. His intention was to take exactly what he needed and nothing more. He also wanted it all in a backpack that weighed no more than 25 pounds. Researching the lightest weight and best quality space blankets, cooking equipment, water filtration system, dehydrated food, navigation equipment and other essentials kept him busy all winter, and, as a result, he encountered no problems in the wilderness. In fact, he had a great time and will probably go again next year. Whether or not hiking and camping is your cup of tea (it's definitely not mine!), the way Carl prepared can teach us all something about our mental and physical preparation for an emergency that may extend for weeks or longer. Carl agreed to share his equipment list, which may be found in Appendix A. Anyone can assemble a 25-pound backpack with survival gear, whether you end up needing it or not. Of course, making provision for children, the elderly, companion animals, and others who can't do their own preparation needs to be part of your plan. There are many good books that will help with the specifics of survival preparation, and I've listed some of these in the resources list. Here, we're concerned with more general types of preparation for the coming shift.

Whether you create a simpler, more satisfying lifestyle before or after an event that displaces you from your home is up to you. In the first instance it will be your choice; in the second, it will be a necessity. Either scenario is okay, but at least think about what for you and your household would constitute simple living. While it isn't necessarily simpler to grow your own food, for example, it's a great way to reconnect with the natural world and to have your own supply of nutritious vegetables, fruits, and possibly nuts and seeds. Gardening is also very satisfying and life-giving. The lost art of canning may be a part of your future, as you store away what you need for the winter months. Sprouting can keep you supplied with high nutrition food that takes only a few days to grow. Again, good books on these subjects abound, and I've listed a couple of my favorites in the resources list.

A really interesting book is novelist Barbara Kingsolver's *Animal, Vegetable, Miracle: A Year of Food Life.* It's her own story of how she, her husband, and two daughters took a year out on an old family farm to live off the land and their own labor. They set some ground rules: to grow virtually all their own food and eat only what was in season (no asparagus in August, for example), to buy from or exchange with local producers whatever they needed to fill in their diet, to share the chores, and make the whole experience worthwhile and enjoyable for all of them. They encountered some surprises along the way, as you might imagine, but the whole family found the experience very fulfilling, and it bonded them closer together. They now have a much deeper appreciation for what it takes to bring food to the table and to make it a nurturing, nourishing center of their lives together. They also discovered anew Earth's natural rhythms and grew in appreciation and respect for her abundance.

This is what I mean by simplicity—adopting a lifestyle that is not less work necessarily but is more life-giving, harmonious, and natural, one that strengthens human relationships with Earth and other species, as well as within the community. Not everyone can retreat to a farm and live off the land, but a great many people can keep small gardens, even in the city, and community gardens are great ways to share the labor and its fruits, as well as building community spirit. The organic and biodynamic food movements are growing by leaps and bounds, as people are willing to pay a little more for food they know is free of toxins. Local co-ops and farmers' markets are becoming more popular, too. The one we use is excellent, and in the summer you have to come early to get the best, freshest produce, eggs, and meat. Only goods that are produced by the sellers may be offered there, which is a real advantage. You get to know the vendors and what they'll have coming in in the next few weeks.

Recently my husband and I toured several local farms practicing sustainable food production. One of the most interesting was Infinity Farm that uses the Rudolph Steiner principles of biodynamics to grow and harvest food. Biodynamics goes beyond organic farming in three ways: viewing the farm as a living ecosystem that can be made largely self-sufficient; using biodynamic nutrients (herbal and animal) to support plant growth; and (to me the most interesting) following not only Earth's natural rhythms but also the planetary influences of sun, moon, planets, and stars on plant growth and production. Farmer Jon at Infinity Farm told us about an experiment in which he planted seeds on four successive days, three of them aligned with the natural rhythms and one not. The first three plants turned out to be twice as large as the last, planted during a solar eclipse! The ancients knew and used these cosmic influences to good effect as well. One aspect of the Mayan calendar was and still is used for agricultural purposes to ensure the most auspicious growing and harvesting seasons.

Most communities now have natural foods or farmers' markets of one kind or another. Buying and eating locally is becoming a trend, as gas prices skyrocket and people are concerned about the quality of imported foods. Next time you reach for a 4.4 ounce carton of blueberries from Chili that costs $4.00, think about buying fresh ones at the local market next summer and canning or freezing them for the winter.

We need to learn again the knowledge and skills of the ancients who lived close to the land. Following the solar and lunar cycles, the natural rhythms of the seasons, is part of human experience. When I stood at the grand Mayan temple Chitzen Itza in the Yucatan where the Serpent of Light moves down the nine levels of the pyramid on Spring Equinox, I was awestruck by how much our ancestors knew about time and the cycles of the cosmos. When the Serpent of Light, the male kundalini energy of the Sun, appeared to fertilize the female kundalini energy of the Earth, it was time to plant the seeds that would be harvested in later months to feed the community. It was something the community could count on, and despite our erratic weather, unless we get a pole shift, we can, too. At sacred sites I've visited all over the world—Stonehenge, the temples along the Nile, Newgrange in Ireland, Maes Howe on Orkney Island off northern Scotland, Chaco Canyon in New Mexico, "America's Stonehenge" in New Hampshire, and in dozens of other places I know about, similar events happen, incontrovertible evidence that the ancients established these sites to coincide with the movement of the heavens. "As above, so below" is the message of "on Earth as it is in Heaven."

The high priests, who were astrologers and adepts, chose carefully and well the energetically charged places on the Earth's grid system where they would build their temples. These places and what happened there during the seasonal ceremonies charged and amplified the energy of the Earth, connecting her grids with the etheric grids that join all life at every level throughout the cosmos. When you stand on those sites today, you can feel the surge of energy and your own connection with the Earth and the Universe. A sacred crystal I placed at three spots within the inner circle at Stonehenge was hot to the touch when I picked it up on an overcast 50° morning. Earth is alive!

The knowledge and wisdom of the ancients is readily available to us today, and I strongly recommend that you make learning it a part of your preparation for the shift. Again, check the resources list in Appendix B for good information. If Earth experiences a pole shift, we'll need to learn to orient ourselves by the stars rather than by a compass or GPS satellite, or we'll be all turned around. The ancients–and indigenous people even today–also knew how to read nature's signs, which signaled coming severe weather conditions, a late spring or harvest, unusual animal, bird, insect, and fish behavior indicating it was time to move on, and other indications of how the natural world was changing or providing the conditions needed for sustaining life for the community. Now we're hearing about all kinds of strange patterns which tell us the shift is near. The migratory patterns of birds, sea creatures, and wildlife are becoming erratic, indicating their confusion about safe places to feed or raise their young.

I had a personal experience with the migratory problems of cetaceans in the summer of 2004. I was guided to take a very large cluster crystal to Orcas Island off the coast of Seattle, Washington, and drop it in the ocean for the Orca whales and dolphins. The guidance included a date range in early June and the particular cluster crystal to take. The rest was up to me. I'm used to receiving strange requests like this, and so are some of my friends. Five others, when they heard about this mission, spontaneously offered to accompany me. The six of us gathered on that beautiful island the night before the crystal drop and prepared with spiritual energy healing, prayer, and meditation. We felt that the crystal was to anchor energy for the Orcas and dolphins and in the future to guide them to their summer feeding and breeding grounds. The next day we went out on a commercial sightseeing boat and learned that just the night before the three pods of Orcas who shared this habitat had returned from their winter migration. Coincidence? I don't think so. We picked the spot to drop the crystal in the ocean and sensed that it offered a constant beacon of light for the animals to orient themselves. Soon afterwards our boat was surrounded by whales swimming alongside us and acting as though they were thanking us for the crystal. This episode, which brought our group great joy and a sense of connection to these highly intelligent mammals, illustrates that humans can work together with other species to bring about the changes needed for all of us to survive.

The flip side of this was a program I saw recently on public television about the migratory patterns of polar bears, who are in great peril because of the melting of the polar caps. Many are drowning or dying of starvation as their world changes around them. They have not yet learned to adapt and are having to walk miles inland to find food. The horrible site of a polar bear in an Alaskan town trying to pull a fast-food bag out of a pile of burning trash seared my heart. We cannot continue behavior that forces these animals and countless other species to perish as a result.

Part of our own preparation is to observe and connect with our local wildlife. People who live close to the land know when something is out of whack with their environment because they are so familiar with plant and wildlife patterns. *The Farmers' Almanac* used to offer guidance on weather patterns and animal behavior to help farmers determine what and when to plant. Now we urban-suburbanites haven't a clue what kinds of wildlife even share our habitats. Study yours and make notes about what seems to be shifting. These shifts are important clues as to what might lie ahead. Get your children or grandchildren involved in studying their ecosystems. My son, who's 38, still remembers his high school ecology class that tested local groundwater and discovered sources of pollution, then advocated for change. All of our lives as well as that of local species depend on our understanding and responding to changes in our environment.

Just as the animal kin-dom is essential to our ecosystems, so is the vegetable or plant kin-dom. In order to grow food, we need to know what kinds of plants will survive and thrive in our gardens. Last summer, our first in our new home, we discovered loads of berry-laden blackberry bushes on our property. Harvesting these as they became ripe and freezing some for the fall gave us a sense of satisfaction and connection to the land for which we are stewards. We share the sense of indigenous peoples that we do not own the land; it exists for all local species and for itself. We may use it to create abundant food for ourselves, enough to share with the animals, birds, and insects but must not strip it of its capacity to provide for future generations. Over-farming land, then moving on and doing it again has been a human pattern. Land needs time to refresh and restore itself.

Our former ranch in northern New Mexico, a beautiful, wild place not well suited for humans, although they had lived there off and on for at least a thousand years, is an example of over-farming. With the purchase of the ranch we received a lease on nearly 1000 acres of BLM (Bureau of Land Management) land, for which we paid $10 a year to the federal government. In the past ranchers had run cattle on this land, as our neighbors still were doing, and stripped it of grass and nutrients. We arranged to restore the grasslands and worked with government programs that supported this goal. After we sold the ranch a few years later, the new owners began running cattle again, depleting the resources so that ten acres or more were needed to support one cow. Add this practice together with traditional drought and fires, and the future of states like New Mexico, Arizona, Utah, and Nevada looks grim.

As stewards of the land we live on and are surrounded by, we need to learn how to replenish the ecosystem so that it will support future generations of life. Right now at home we have a family of five deer who visit us regularly. As more and more of their habitat is eaten up by development and drought, such wildlife will compete for food and eventually birth rates will decline as the land can no longer sustain them. This land was theirs long before it was ours.

Native plants do better than non-native species. That's pretty basic. Yet people persist in planting grass lawns in areas of drought and bringing in exotic, invasive species that take over the native plant life. If you've ever seen the devastating affects of kudzu choking out trees, shrubs, and wildlife in the South, you know what

I mean. Ornamental plants may be attractive, but if they spread and become a canker on the land, they can wreak havoc.

Consider taking a class for local gardeners to learn about your native plants and how to create a sustainable garden, including edible plants. As weather patterns change and some locations get colder and others warmer, you'll need to know what will and won't do well in the coming years. This assumes that you'll stay put. Just as we need to be prepared to migrate, we also need to plan for the kind of climate that will come to us. There are tons of good resources on growing your own food, including herbs and sprouts that you can grow indoors. Everyone can create part or all of their own food sources, especially if they band together to create community gardens.

It's also time to recognize that we're going to have to eat less meat and fish. Our ancestors were natural vegetarians, eating nuts, seeds, grains, and fruit. We can still sustain a diet on those highly nutritional substances, although finding them in the future will be a challenge unless we plant the trees, shrubs and seeds that produce them. Over-fishing our seas is a global problem, as is the toxicity of our oceans, rivers, and lakes. Meat from cattle, hogs, and poultry is not only expensive to produce but also uses up most of the world's grains that could be used to feed the starving. As weather conditions and fuel scarcity make grain production more difficult, shortages are anticipated, with worldwide famine a real possibility. Reducing or eliminating our meat consumption can avert that coming crisis. We don't need nearly as much protein as we consume. According to those who have studied blood types, those of us with Type O blood need more protein than those with A and B blood types, but soy products, nuts, and eggs can provide most of what we need. Eating more nutritious foods will also improve our health.

We're learning the ancient wisdom of natural products to aid in healing as well. Herbal remedies, essential oils made from pure distillations of plants, and other products from nature should be part of anyone's first aid kit, especially if shortages of prescription drugs and lack of medical treatment threaten your health and that of your family. There are natural or homeopathic remedies for most common ailments. Good books on this subject abound. I have a goodly supply of essential oils like peppermint, lavender, oregano, and cedar to restore and promote healing. It takes only a few drops to make a difference, and these oils are easily portable and simple to use. I gave one of my friends a business idea recently: make up emergency natural medicine kits and market them on eBay and Craig's List! If she doesn't move on this idea, maybe one of you readers will.

If you're unable to produce and stockpile your own food, maybe you'd like to stock up on dehydrated foods. Dehydration preserves the nutritional value of the original foods far better than canning, for example. These food sources are also easy to store and use. Try an internet search for dehydrated foods, and you'll be surprised at how many sites come up that offer good quality nutrition at a reasonable price. Some of these are pre-packaged to provide the caloric levels and nutritional values needed per person, so just order and stockpile what you may need for your family. You don't need much space to ensure a ready food supply for weeks or months if stored according to directions. Most sources for these foods also sell equipment and materials that help you make your own dehydrated food. Of course, you'll need water to hydrate the food, cooking oil, and a source of heat, but you'll have the basics covered. If this meets your needs better than growing your own, by all means stock up on enough to keep you fed for at least three months—the time it might take to migrate, grow food, or connect with a community that could provide what you'd need.

A clean water source is also essential in case of emergency, more so than food. We can only last a few days without water but can go a couple of weeks without food. Whether you'll be staying put in your own place or migrating, you'll need to figure out how to get enough water, about a gallon a day per person. A good filtration system for rainwater, local ponds or streams, even water from your toilet tanks and hot water heater, will be necessary. Again, there are many ways to filter water for drinking, and Appendix B contains a few good sources of this kind of information.

Temporary housing may also be necessary. Different kinds of tents, sleeping bags, and shelters may be investigated and kept on hand. If you're a camper, you already have this equipment. Make sure it's suited for the climate you'll be traveling to or live in now. If you need to rebuild after a disaster of some kind and can't depend on local governments or neighbors to help, you may be able to find abandoned structures that can be converted to housing. Natural structures like caves—be sure they are uninhabited by snakes, bats, and bears—and tree houses can be utilized. If you have a camper or RV, you'll be all set—at least until you run out of gas or your waste tank fills up. Again, banding together with others in similar circumstances should be your best bet.

Rather than going into a great deal of detail about these kinds of survival issues, as there are many excellent sources of information already available, I'm just raising your consciousness about the kinds of things you need to be thinking about and preparing for as part of your survival on a physical level. Hope for the best and prepare for the worst may be good advice.

In that regard, in the group that gathered for the Epiphany Weekend conversation in January were two sisters who have developed a retreat center in northwestern Tennessee. There, on seventy acres, our friends have been preparing for years for the kinds of Earth changes and emergencies talked about. Instead of learning about this for the first time, as some of us were doing, Our friends had been living off the grid, stockpiling food and seeds, keeping horses, gardening, canning, sprouting, and teaching others how to get ready for the future. They are all set up for temporary guests, with comfortable sleeping quarters in a bunk house, communal cooking on a wood stove and outdoor fire pit, a latrine, several potable water sources and lots of canned goods they make themselves when they find essential foods on sale. They teach others basic survival and independent living skills. Sharing chores in community is different from having to do everything yourselves. That's one of the big benefits of large families and communal living. Sitting around the fire at night telling stories and sharing experiences make our HDTV's seem unnecessary. A deck of cards or a board game could likewise entertain a family for hours. In fact, I remember many evenings from my childhood when that was the case. A game of bridge, poker, or Hearts requires no material investment and returns lots of fun and camaraderie.

The retreat center in Tennessee reminds me of the family gatherings with my mother's relatives in rural Michigan, of my aunt catching and killing a chicken for dinner (which I couldn't eat because I'd seen its demise), drinking milk fresh from a cow, and using an outhouse rather than a flush toilet. I'm citified through and through but know if I had to I could live a low tech life. I've done it already and appreciate what it has to offer. If we can see what we've gained from a simpler lifestyle rather than what we've lost, we'll be way ahead of most in our high tech culture who've never known anything else.

Our Tennessee friends remind us that there's a practical application side to preparing for the Great Shift. A dress rehearsal is a great idea. Get together a group of friends and family and share thoughts on how to cope and thrive and create community. Even a week-long camping trip with your family or a few friends in which you all spend time figuring out what you'll need and gathering it together, packing it, using it in the field, and evaluating what you needed more or less of is good practice for getting ready to leave home in an emergency.

You don't have to have land in order to live sustainably. You can create a similar kind of lifestyle and experience with family, neighbors, or friends anywhere. A friend in metro Detroit told me about an incident a couple of summers ago when the whole area lost power for nearly three days. Realize that this meant no electricity for running water, cooking or air conditioning, no telephones, TV, computers, or other technology. Food in freezers began to thaw. Neighbors, all in the same boat, began to gather at each others' houses to hold communal barbecues, each family contributing what would spoil if it weren't used up. My friend checked on her neighbors to make sure they were all right and had what they needed. People shared their pet food, over-the-counter meds, and beverages with each other. Rather than holding back and hoarding, not knowing how long the emergency would last, they treated the situation like a big party and got to know their neighbors better. The resulting relationships have lasted, and these folks developed a sense of security that if something happened again they had a community for support and survival. Instead of going into fear they went into the heart and pulled out love and joy. It was a great lesson for my friend, who was new to the neighborhood, and provided a model of how to get along in the future.

If you don't know your neighbors, now is the time to meet them. My husband, son, and I moved into a new subdivision last year. One of the first things we did was to hold a house blessing, inviting all the neighbors as well as friends. Our previous neighborhood was well organized through its homeowners' association. We had directories of all the families, their kids and pets, monthly social gatherings, book and gardening clubs, and a Yahoo! Group online. That online network was especially effective. It served to notify people of somebody's missing child or pet, a neighborhood break-in, a car or car-seat for sale, an invitation to play volleyball on the local court, the location of the Saturday night potluck, a recommended plumber or painter, and so on. If your neighborhood doesn't have such a group, I strongly advise you to gather some neighbors and create one, as it's the fastest and best way to notify each other of what's happening around you. In an emergency, these are the people that can go to each other's aid the fastest and, aside from family, have the most incentive to provide mutual support.

In addition, as one friend suggested, working through your homeowners' association to create a disaster preparedness plan would be a very valuable exercise. This could include an evacuation plan, a gathering place in an emergency, a notification system, and list of resources. Condo and townhouse associations in denser areas can do likewise. Rural communities can work through their local co-ops, churches, and lodges or create their own community groups.

Speaking of churches, in which I spent many years, there are networks already in place, like prayer chains or call lists, that could pass the word around quickly in case of emergency. In addition to the usual home visitation groups, churches could form emergency preparedness teams to check on members and also the wider community. Churches and temples are natural gathering places for people in emergencies, and their congregations can provide needed community leadership alongside local government.

Other natural affinity groups at work sites, schools, and colleges could institute emergency plans as well, coordinating these with other local groups so that the needs of their constituents could be met without delay and confusion. Unfortunately, after many incidents of shootings on campuses, such as Columbine High School and Virginia Tech University, such plans exist in situations requiring security in a hurry. These could be expanded to cover a whole range of situations, like explosions, hurricanes and tornados, earthquakes, and the like. Tying these to the kinds of plans that organizations like the American Red Cross and the Humane Society of the US already have in place will provide the coordination and effective deployment of personnel and materials needed. The military, municipalities, government agencies and many other organizations already have such plans and could teach the rest of the world how to create coordinated plans and make them operational.

Katrina survivors learned that you can't wait for the government to save you and that you have to save yourselves as well as others who can't do so on their own. Leadership in disaster preparedness is much needed at this time. Perhaps you'll be inspired to train for this and implement plans within the organizations you are a part of. Be sure to include all the kinds of situations that could arise and focus on those most likely.

No one but intuitives and psychics could have predicted the 9/11 World Trade Center disaster, but many communities are now better prepared because that happened. Let's not wait until something devastating comes along before we get ready. Expect that in these changing times something will come up to trigger the activation of the plan you create on the path through 2012.

CHAPTER SEVEN: THRIVE IN A NEW ECONOMY

Is a Global Financial Collapse in Our Future?

Despite what economists and politicians say to the contrary, the U.S. economy has slowed to a recession, and if the U.S. is in recession, a large part of the interconnected rest of the world will soon be, too. This recession is fueled by a major decline in housing prices around the country, the related mortgage and credit crises, and soaring oil prices. The economy also has suffered from the huge trade deficit and the resulting decline of the dollar against world currencies. States are cutting budgets and services, companies are slashing jobs or going bankrupt, and this is just the tip of the iceberg.

According to numerous accounts, the world has already reached peak oil, which means that demand is likely to exceed supply from here on out. Oil recently hit a new high price point at nearly $150 a barrel. Since the world's economies and consumers depend on fossil fuels for just about everything, this is not good news. The U.S. economy is built around oil. In the face of high oil prices for the foreseeable future, airlines are cutting way back on flights and personnel and tacking on charges for checking baggage, and the auto industry seems to finally have gotten the message that fuel economy is now a top priority for people. Public transportation services are feeling the strain of increased ridership, while resorts and restaurants are experiencing reduced traffic. Gas prices are causing families to cut back on discretionary spending, and there's no end in sight. It feels like a house of cards has started to shake in the winds of change.

We are rapidly approaching a possible worldwide financial collapse led by oil prices and demand. We're way behind in the research and development of alternative energy sources. So-called "clean" coal and nuclear power plants are considered by business to be acceptable alternatives, but people don't want them in their communities. Remember the movie *The China Syndrome* with Jack Lemmon and Jane Fonda? That near-disaster at a power plant near you could happen. It did happen in Chernobyl, Ukraine, in 1986, and this once-thriving city is now a ghost-town. The nuclear industry still hasn't figured out how to dispose of waste safely. In addition, it draws upon precious water resources for cooling its plants, water that becomes heavy and unusable.

So that leaves natural resources like solar and wind power as the most promising sources, yet we are decades behind in production. Without huge incentives and billions poured into new development of safe, reliable, renewable, cheap energy sources, by 2012 we may be back to the low tech lifestyle of our great-grandparents. That's not all bad, as I pointed out in the last chapter, but it would be nice to have a choice. Living off the grid may become a way of life because the grid is down—temporarily or permanently.

Worldwide shortages not only of fuel but also of food, water, and other necessities are to be expected. People who foresee that are stocking up now and preparing in the kinds of ways discussed earlier. But there's another dimension to life leading up to 2012 and beyond that we need to look at more closely. That is what may happen to individual and family financial resources in the face of a major economic collapse. As a Certified Financial Planner for twenty-one years, I had a private practice in New Jersey during the '80's and remember well the day in October, 1987 when the stock market dropped precipitously for no apparent reason. Panicky clients called, wanting to know what to do, and frankly I hadn't a clue. Like other financial advisors, I then believed that the U.S. stock market was a great investment for the long-term investor. I could cite statistics going back sixty years showing that the average annual return in stocks exceeded that of bonds or money market instruments, which typically lost ground to inflation. But in the face of a sudden, steep decline, I was as nervous as my clients. Did I trust the system to recover or was this the beginning of some kind of global economic catastrophe? Sucking it up and choosing at that time to trust the system and its history, I advised more than one client to hold on and ride it out. Those who did recovered financially in a few months. Those who didn't lost a lot of money. This time it may be the other way around.

I retired my CFP license in 2005, so I no longer give investment advice, but that experience taught me humility and caution. No investment is without risk of one kind or another. The conventional wisdom is to diversify risk across classes of assets and time frames, but the kind of portfolio that's worked well in the past is not, I believe, going to do well for the foreseeable future.

People who expected their home equity to provide a comfortable retirement didn't take into account the potential for a major decline in housing prices. Fixed interest investments return net losses after inflation and taxes. Stock market volatility scares off the public, and commodities can be risky, too. What are people to do with their money these days—if they have any?

Take Charge of Your Personal Finances

Not going into fear about loss of financial security is and will continue to be a challenge. While we may feel secure spiritually, the thought of not having enough money causes great anxiety and stress. It's connected with the fear of losing control of your life. In order to shift this fear into a positive emotional vibration, take charge of your personal financial situation now by making lifestyle decisions that can improve your financial circumstances.

One big move could be to pay down debt, especially auto loans and credit cards. Another would be to reduce spending as much as possible. With the credit crisis in this country well under-way, the over consuming population would do well to reign in and conserve. The U. S. Congress, in an election year, passed another big tax cut that put $300 to $1200 into the hands of consumers, which the feds hoped would be spent to stimulate the sagging economy. My advice when a windfall of any kind comes your way is to pay down your highest interest rate bills first, thus freeing up monthly cash to pay them down further.

Unlike conservative talk-show hosts who advise eliminating debt entirely, I still think an affordable home mortgage, with the tax deduction it brings, is acceptable for most people—just don't draw all of your home equity out to spend on things that don't improve the value of the home, or you'll find yourself in the unenviable position of owing the bank money if you have to—or are able to—sell your home. Negative amortization of home loans will keep people trapped in debt and in their homes for years to come, unless and until the housing market recovers.

If you have second homes and large toys, like boats and sports cars that you can do without, consider selling and consolidating your funds. If you can't get much for the goods you can do without, you may want to give them away and claim a tax deduction. Besides, non profits, especially those dealing with people's and animals' basic needs, are being hard-hit these days, and it's only going to get worse. Remember those in need, as an essential part of the new consciousness is that all will have enough. In the interconnected web, no one can be left behind. Those of us who have more than enough will have to share with those who don't, and after the Great Shift we've do it gladly, not grudgingly.

In addition to paying down debt and selling or giving away what you can do without, consider investing in some goods that will aid you through the coming shift, particularly if times get hard and shortages are common. I'm not talking about hoarding and protecting your stash with guns—that's exactly the consciousness we need to leave behind—but rather prudently preparing your lists of essentials for you, your family, neighbors, friends, and those you'll care for in the event of difficult times. Again, these might include renewable energy sources for your home and car, alternative transportation if gas is unavailable, such as bicycles or a horse and wagon, if you live in the country. Walking is always good, and improving your physical condition is an important part of our preparation for what's ahead. You'll need a reliable water source and good, nourishing food. Low-tech items like hand-cranked radios, can openers, and other non-electric kitchen gadgets are a good idea to have on hand. Check out www.Lehmans.com for these kinds of items. There are many books and websites now, listed in Appendix B, with lists of items to purchase to be prepared for an emergency, if shortages of goods and services are a part of our future. The point is that purchasing these kinds of items may be a better use of your funds than where you have them now.

If in the future we do have a worldwide economic collapse, monetary systems will be affected. It's possible that the currencies we use now may lose considerable value. Recession turns to depression when the economy slows and inflation increases as a result of shortages of vital products and services. The global depression of the 1930's could be repeated or worse. Many countries have experienced runaway inflation and the deflation of their currency, so that could conceivably be something we experience. In that case, there are four important strategies you may use to get what you need: bartering, buying locally, creating micro-businesses, and communal living.

Bartering

Bartering for goods and services is an age-old economic system that is still in use around the world because it works. Trading what you have, make, or do for something you need or could use is well understood by people of all ages. It can be done on a very small scale or a very large one. Think about all the goods and services you could bring to a trade, like caring for a neighbor's children in exchange for using their lawn mower or fixing someone's bike in exchange for a meal. People barter naturally. When someone offers you something, your generous nature wants to reciprocate. Last week friends brought us a big bowl of homemade chili and corn bread out of the goodness of their hearts. As soon as our garden tomatoes are ready, they'll be first on our list to receive nature's bounty.

Bartering is about reciprocity, equivalency, mutuality. You get into a relationship when you're bartering rather than using a monetary medium, which creates more distance in the transaction. As you think about it, you'll find all kinds of opportunities in your daily life to create trades or to barter. Practice bartering until you get the hang of it and see how easy it is to operate this way without money. If you believe what you're trading is worth more than what the person is offering, try getting them to sweeten the deal by asking what else they can include.

Barter is easiest when it's done among people who know and trust each other, but it's not necessary to limit it that way. Internet services like www.craigslist.com, which operates in most metropolitan areas, can include items and services to barter with what you want in return. It's an efficient means of exchange. Just put an ad up with a couple of pictures or a description of what you want and what you're offering, and see how many "hits" you get. If people believe what they have is worth more than what is offered, that's where bargaining skill comes in. It's important to stay in the heart when bartering, remembering that good will and a positive attitude toward the process will allow you and your trading partners to rise above anger, fear, and greed, and develop a good relationship. That's really important and absolutely crucial for the higher consciousness we're working towards. By taking money out of the equation, sometimes people are even more generous in bartering.

People who don't have much money or disposable income use the barter system all the time. I use it frequently to exchange healing sessions with friends. Bartering also has tax advantages, if there's no income to declare.

Barter can be used in business situations as well as in your personal lives. A friend recently told us a story about how his company was approached years ago by a Russian company that wanted computer parts. They didn't have the cash to pay for their order and instead sent a load of mink coats (this was before people stopped wearing fur in support of animals)! Through a contact, the friend was able to sell the coats to a dealer for more than the parts were worth. It cost him some time and effort, but he made out all right. Trading your business services is even easier than trading goods. Maybe eBay could add a bartering section for people who'd like a wider network in which to do exchanges. It can be creative and fun as well as practical. So start using a barter system, get good at it, and you may be able to teach bartering to others.

In addition to a barter system, some communities have developed their own currencies and issue and use these in place of the national currency. A nearby town, Carrboro, NC, has Carrboro Bucks that are used for local shopping and services. Any community could develop such a system, and this may become quite likely if the national system breaks down. During the Civil War, Confederate currency was viable, while afterwards it was used in outhouses. Money has only the value people give to it, after all. It represents value rather than having intrinsic value. The idea of a local currency could benefit from exploration now, so that an alternative system could be ready to put in place as needed. Just as the European Union countries are adopting the Euro—with a few notable exceptions, like Great Britain—communities at all levels of complexity might find their own tradable currency easier to manage than a barter system, which is cruder and more personal. The point is that if the U.S. dollar or other currency you are using loses its value, you and your community can create a substitute. That may not make you feel any better if you lose your savings, but in the new economy that emerges out of the Great Shift, I believe the present inequities in the old paradigm systems will be corrected.

Buying Locally and Supporting Your Neighbors

The second strategy for the coming age which is a good practice regardless of the state of the economy is buying locally. Supporting your local merchants and food producers will enable them to stay in business and continue to serve you, as well as promoting good relationships. "Locavores", those who advocate buying and eating locally, are growing in numbers. The issue that comes up when people talk about buying locally is whether they can get the same or better quality at the same or lower price than at a big box store that's part of a national or international chain. Just as we pay a bit more for organic food because of its nutritional value, we may have to pay extra to our local merchants. A novelist friend makes a practice of buying from her local bookstore that sponsors her readings and promotes her books rather than buying online or from one of the national chains. If she and others like her don't do so, the small, personal stores will go out of business.

Do you think the large chains will care about your inconvenience if they decide to pull out of your community because their bottom lines don't meet corporate expectations? In the same way that mega-corporations outsource local jobs to areas where labor costs are considerably lower than the U.S., even pulling out of towns built around their manufacturing operations, big business is not built on quality personal relationships, whereas small business has to be.

In the new economy of higher consciousness, people and the Earth matter. They are not to be exploited for profit. That old paradigm is dying hard right now. So get to know your local vendors and services and support them with your business. If they're bureaucratic and not committed to excellent service, vote with your feet and your pocketbook. Go elsewhere and let them know, courteously, why. It may be inconvenient, but you'll make your point and feel better about your decision.

Vital public services, like health care, education, and social services, are particularly poorly run in this country and, for the most part, perpetually under-funded. Working with them to bring about positive change is challenging. If you encounter service workers with an attitude, be empathetic to what they must deal with every day. Choose your words carefully and respectfully with the intent to heal, not harm.

Buying goods locally can also improve the quality and pricing of what you're purchasing, as you support the local businesses. Buying in bulk and joining with neighbors and friends to make larger purchases can also get you better prices. Use your bargaining and bartering skills to do so, something you can't do in big box stores. As you know, locally grown food from your farmers' market or stocked in chain stores is generally fresher and better quality, too. We have a local dairy here in the Chapel Hill area, Maple View Dairy, which makes the best vanilla ice cream I've ever eaten—it's rich without being too sweet. You can purchase it at a number of local stores or drive out to the dairy on a summer afternoon for a double dip cone! That's a treat I hope will still be available to us as we move into a higher reality! Another local dairy farm we recently visited has become organic and is selling to a national chain, making it easy to find in stores. The farmer found the conversion from traditional to organic practices difficult but now wouldn't go back. His farm is nearly self-sustainable in its practices and his products are high quality. He feels good about his business and what he's building for his children and the community.

The early ecology movement made a strong point of encouraging people to buy locally. Books like the *Small is Beautiful* series by British economist and ecologist E. F. Schumacher, first published in 1973, led the sustainability movement in that earlier generation, and they are still relevant today. We can learn much from the work that's been done within the deep ecology movement over the last nearly forty years. Another of my favorite books, *For the Common Good: Redirecting the Economy Toward Community, the Environment and a Sustainable Future* by economist Herman Daly and theologian John F. Cobb, published in 1989, fueled my own interest in the sustainability movement from a spiritual perspective. Daly and Cobb argued that the common good must become the standard for business and the economy. In our spiritual work, we also ask for the outcome which is for the highest good of each and all. Why wouldn't we ask the same for the kind of world we want to live in in the future? A world transformed would put serving all, including the Earth, above making a profit. Yes, there must be incentives for people to offer a high level of products and services, but in the new economy greed won't be a factor.

Just as the Asian Tsunami of 2004 caused a worldwide opening of hearts and an outpouring of compassion on a large scale, people love to help on smaller scales, too. In my work as a minister I saw how generous people could be when they felt the suffering of others. One project involved an interfaith community council with representatives from local religious organizations and social services to integrate efforts to serve the community's residents in need.

As you know, many communities across the U.S. hold an annual spring or fall tour of homes to show off historical or beautiful properties. Our council decided to sponsor another kind of spring tour of homes. Getting permission from several of the people our congregation had helped, we got a group together to experience what it was like to live in hot trailers in 90 degree heat or not to have your own running water. This was in the mid-'90's, and there were still people in this wealthy community who had to run a hose from a neighbor's house to get water for their needs. This tour of homes was a real eye opener. Those who went with us were appalled at what they saw and began to address several of the problems they encountered. Out of this came an organization that advocated successfully for public water access for all households. This happened within two years of our tour. Another group pressed utility companies to make landlords provide adequate heating and cooling systems in substandard housing, so that low income residents didn't have to pay huge sums of money for electricity. People who rent dumps because that's all they can afford end up being evicted even from those when they can't pay their inflated utility bills. They need advocates. Unfortunately, we didn't make a lot of progress on this issue because the power—pun intended—was in the hands of the utilities and the landlords. But we did create a team that offered home repairs and improvements and another that helped out in emergencies.

You can't love your neighbor as yourself if you don't know your neighbor. The question becomes "Who is my neighbor?" Defining our neighbors too narrowly separates us from the rest of the world. When we speak about the common good, we mean what's good for all, not just some. When we really understand that, we'll not be far from the kin-dom of God, to paraphrase Jesus.

So getting to know and care about your neighbors is a part of the economic strategy I've been talking about. When people feel that they are known and cared about, they respond with their own love and generosity. People without financial resources have much to offer and teach those of us who are relatively well-off, whether it's a homemade pie, a song, or a word of advice. In the new economy we will not separate ourselves into the "haves" and "have nots", yet with the current geopolitical and economic systems, that's just what has happened. Caring about our neighbors locally and around the world means treating everyone as well as we'd like to be treated. That means building relationships of mutuality and trust. If you see yourself as doing all the giving or being always on the receiving end, you're allowing an energetic as well as economic imbalance that will cause resentment. Caring for others includes allowing reciprocity in a relationship. When you allow those you give to to give back to you, everyone benefits. That's the beauty of the barter system, for example, and of dealing with local businesses and merchants, who are your neighbors.

A Canadian friend of mine calls the U.S. economy "rapacious," meaning grasping or preying on the weak or powerless, and at its worst it is that. But when business is built around relationships, the power imbalance is diminished. When people of integrity deal honestly and fairly with their customers and employees, standing behind their products and services, it seems unusual these days, doesn't it? That's the result of bottom-line driven big business, whether it's in health care or the auto industry or cell phone service. How many times have you wanted to scream in frustration and anger when dealing with "customer service"? For me, it's become a test of my ability to remain patient and centered in the heart. A friendly rather than belligerent attitude shifts the energy and improves the outcome.

Creating Micro-Businesses

One solution to the problems of dealing with large, impersonal businesses is to deal with or create micro-businesses, small scale operations that can consist of just one or a handful of persons. In fact, home-based businesses and workers are dramatically on the rise, as people want more flexibility in their schedules and companies want to cut costs. Working from home solves child-care issues, reduces commuting costs and related carbon emissions, lowers clothing budgets, and eliminates expensive lunches eaten in restaurants. The neighborhood we lived in before this one had at least one person in every other household, it seemed, working from home. Some had their own businesses, like lining up expert witnesses for trial lawyers, computer consulting, making custom-made golf clubs, and giving tennis lessons on the community courts. Others worked for companies from home—one consulted for a university admissions office, another sold advertising for a journal, and a third did funds development work for the local hospital. The home office has become as important a room in the home these days as the family room—more important than the dining room used for special occasions. If you have a computer and high-speed internet, you can have a home-based business or become a telecommuter.

Your own home-based business is just one example of a micro-business. Interestingly enough, micro-economies have grown in third world countries, where, thanks to innovative lending practices, individuals can get small loans to start a simple business. A woman in an African village might purchase a cell phone with her loan and make money by charging people to use it. A family might buy a cow or a pair of goats or a few chickens and produce dairy products, eggs, and meat not only for themselves but for others to purchase. In poor countries, it doesn't take much to turn someone into a successful entrepreneur—just some ambition, a good idea, and a lender who wants her to succeed. If training is provided, the results improve, of course. See the websites of the Foundation for International Community Assistance, www.villagebanking. org, and The Heifer Project, www.heifer.org, for examples of two great charitable organizations that offer opportunities and ideas for your own participation in global micro-businesses. Communities throughout the U.S. are using the same strategy to empower people to go into business for themselves through targeted lending, training, and community involvement.

Our daughter in Nepal has created several such micro-businesses to support the local economy. The most successful of these, Wild Earth Nepal, uses native herbs and plants gathered in the high Himalayas to make wonderful, unique spa products, like soaps, oils, lotions, and herbal pillows. Carroll's local factory employs dozens of people, and her products are shipped all over the world. Wild Earth supports fair trade practices, ensuring that all involved in the production, distribution, and purchase of the products are treated fairly, as well as adhering to sustainable harvesting practices, so that the herb supply is replenished for the future. The company also contributes to women's and rural economic development in this impoverished country whose daughters are often sent to Thailand to serve as prostitutes for wages to support their families. One visionary, determined person can make a huge difference through a small business like this, and there are thousands of examples of people being pulled out of poverty as a result of efforts to support and sustain micro-businesses.

If we experience the kinds of Earth- and human-caused changes outlined earlier, entrepreneurs will be needed to work smaller, smarter, and friendlier. I can envision someone in each community supporting his or her family or unit by brokering the services and products of the other local entrepreneurs. We're going to be so creative in the higher consciousness that what we imagine, if spiritually aligned, will manifest in no time. It's exciting to contemplate!

A friend in Tucson built a business around creating unique, hand-painted tiles that can be creatively organized and assembled on boards, then framed. She goes around to shows and fairs and is making quite a good living having fun with her artwork. I have one of her early works, a beautiful tile painting of the Madonna in all her glory that replicates a fifteenth-century Spanish painting. To me it represents the fullness of the Divine Feminine radiating her energy and presence into a male-dominated world. Her love shines forth, and you feel her embrace just looking at the painting. That's the kind of work that will be produced by people of higher consciousness in the coming age. It uplifts and supports people, rather than appealing to their lower appetites and addictions. It develops people's gifts and creativity, brings people together, compensates them fairly, and does not exploit the Earth or any of her creatures.

Work after the Great Shift will be satisfying and fun, not drudgery. It will be a communal as well as individual effort, supported at the highest spiritual levels. Contrast this to the work environments of most people around the world who work to live rather than live to work

In the new economy, will we still have available the same or higher levels of technology to assist us in our work? Maybe. And maybe not. Returning to a low tech economy can be a mixed blessing. As an example, when I wrote my Ph.D. dissertation back in 1971, I did it on yellow legal-sized pads of paper. I did all my editing—cross-outs, add-ins, and spell-checking—by hand. Once I was satisfied with the results, I typed the copy with an old manual typewriter, making a carbon copy at the same time. What a slow, messy, and frustrating process! Typos required brushing white-out liquid over the word, waiting for it to dry before proceeding, or retyping the whole page. By the time I wrote my first book, the technology had advanced to electric typewriters with type-over strips for typos, and Xerox machines were available—though expensive—for copies rather than carbon paper. I bought one of the first personal IBM computers in 1982 and struggled with a word processing program called WordStar. I never did master it—too complicated. Thankfully, by the time I wrote my previous book in 2001, Microsoft Word, high-speed internet, and a fax/scan/printer/copier machine made my work as easy as possible. Now, when I travel, I download a document I'm working on to a tiny travel drive, upload it to my laptop, sit in a wireless coffee shop, and I'm in business! In addition, I have a voice recognition program on both computers, Dragon Naturally Speaking, which allows me to speak a document into a microphone and watch the word processor type it in automatically. If you haven't experienced the evolution of technologically assisted writing, you can't appreciate how amazingly simple it now is!

That's just one example of how far we've come technologically in less than forty years. There are dozens of others. I think of the evolution from ice boxes to smart refrigerators that make ice, adjust the temperature, and filter your water, or from clunky telephones to cell phones and personal data assistants that take photos and access the internet. The list goes on. We have come to rely on high tech solutions to make our lives easier and free up more time for work, leisure, or hobbies. What if we had to go back to outhouses and yellow legal pads (if we could find them!)? Would you be able to handle it? If you lived before the explosive technological age, you know you can survive and even thrive if systems break down and cannot be replaced for some time, if ever. At least we'll have the memory and perhaps still the knowledge to recreate some of what we may lose. And who knows? Maybe the Great Shift will result in technologies known in other galaxies and star systems being brought to us. I believe this is possible, even probable. By then we'll have the consciousness to use technology wisely and not allow it to dominate us or become an end rather than a means.

Communal Living

The fourth strategy that will assist the transition to a new economy is to develop a community that will support and sustain you and your family and relieve the pressure on each individual unit to produce enough money to purchase everything a single household needs.

Friends moved to their home in metro Detroit from a condo two years ago. Both are educated professionals and could afford to purchase items needed for their home. However, the husband thought that he might be able to borrow a neighbor's lawn tractor rather than having to lay out a thousand dollars or more for one of his own. He soon found out that people don't do that. Even the offer of a regular supply of fresh fish from this fishing enthusiast wasn't enough to sweeten the deal. These friends are ahead of their time, believing that bartering and sharing so that all have what they need while reducing costs made sense. It does. But you're likely not to find that kind of enlightened thinking in your average neighborhood. The concept of communal living is so important to the coming shift that the next chapter is devoted to it. You'll see the economic as well as the social and spiritual benefits of this as we move on to the subject of creating intentional, sustainable community.

CHAPTER EIGHT: CREATE INTENTIONAL, SUSTAINABLE COMMUNITY

The Importance of Community

The subject of creating intentional, sustainable community is in many ways the most important in this book. Whatever happens through 2012 and afterwards, communities will play a major role in sustaining life on this planet. The human race cannot survive, let alone thrive, when people live in isolation from each other, see themselves as separate, and imagine that the "other", however they definite it, is their enemy. When I visited Bosnia during the war in the mid-nineties and discovered that people who had lived alongside each other peacefully and had no visible differences could end up hating and killing each other, I wondered how that could happen. It happens when people believe that the "other" intends to harm them in some way or just because the other person is different. We draw upon old, reptilian brain energy that thrives on fear and operates at a survival level. This is fed by radical politics, religious fanaticism, propaganda, misunderstanding, and the media, so that people are influenced by the most extreme thoughts and lose perspective.

I saw the same kind of fear, hatred, and narrow-mindedness in Northern Ireland at a peacemaking conference the year after I had been in Bosnia. U.S. Senator George Mitchell led a discussion among leaders of all the Catholic and Protestant political parties which was supposed to promote understanding but instead deteriorated into shouting matches and parochial thinking. People have so much invested in their differences that they can't see their similarities. This is the same old paradigm thinking and behavior we have to get beyond as a species.

Until we are able to move into our heart centers and allow our loving natures to determine our thoughts and actions, we will continue to experience the illusion of separation and the pain that produces. When we are strongly connected to our spiritual core we move beyond our fears and experience the other as a unique expression of the whole self that is one in Spirit. Given all that we are facing as possibilities and probabilities in the next few years, can we get it together and act in our own best interests? That remains to be seen. If we don't, then the Earth may be better off without us. That grim possibility, reflected in the eerie TV program "Life Without Us", is the alternative to the Great Shift to Unity Consciousness. The choice is still ours—at least for a time.

As we have seen, we are all interdependent, physically and spiritually. We have noted that we cannot continue to use natural resources at increasing rates or destroy ecosystems and expect life as usual to continue. And if human-caused changes don't spark dramatic shifts in the next few years, Earth changes will. The handwriting is on the proverbial wall. It is time to form intentional, sustainable community at all levels—local, regional, global, even virtual.

Intentional Community

Intentional communities are those people choose to be part of, often for a particular purpose or focus. One approach is to conceive of the kind of community you would like to be part of and create it through intention and action. Another is to explore an existing community which suits your needs and interests and, if the way is open, choose to join it. Think about the communities you have been or are now a part of and whether belonging to them was your choice or not. Let's start with the family, a community most people have experienced, for better or for worse.

You were born into a family and may think you didn't choose it at all. Have you ever looked at your family and wondered how you got mixed up with these people? At times family members seem like strangers forced to endure each other's idiosyncrasies, like aliens you wouldn't choose to be with if you could help it. Getting over that feeling and learning to love your family members for who they are rather than who you want them to be is part of the process of becoming spiritually mature, loving human beings. Forgiving them and yourself for real and imagined hurts is also a significant part of our spiritual development.

Many believe we do choose our families of origin and the other major players in our lives before we come to the planet for the life lessons and experiences we can offer each other. If you think about this, it may change entirely your own attitude toward the people who gave birth to you, raised you, married you, and became your children or siblings. Even the family is an intentional community, looked at from this perspective. And, in families where the parents loved each other and chose to have children, intention was clearly there, however it worked out. Before the sexual revolution and the women's movement, most people in the dominant culture expected to be married for a lifetime and to have at least a couple of children. That pattern is now in the minority. But since most of us started in one, family is the kind of community with which we are all familiar, offering a way into the subject of intentional community.

Families these days come in all varieties, but a generation or two ago that was different. The big families of the past couple of centuries were communities unto themselves, and if you add in extended families that lived nearby, you had the equivalent of a small town. My own mother came from a family of German-speaking East European immigrants. She was the third of nine children, the only one, to her credit and determination, to finish college. When I was growing up in Detroit, we drove out east of the city on weekends to the rural area where several of her siblings had farms. The grown-ups would chatter, play cards, and prepare a big dinner, while my many cousins of all ages and I would play games outside, like hide-and-go-seek, tag, and kick the can. At night the older ones would tell ghost stories to scare us younger kids. While I wasn't very close to my mother's family—I identified more with my father's side, a professional family who came from England—I learned what it felt like to be part of a large family where everyone was accepted. Everyone was also talked about and criticized, but only within the family. Outsiders weren't privy to the family secrets.

For the most part, my experience with extended family was positive. They were there for us when my older sister died, and we were there for them, lending money as needed, providing work, transportation, and support for several generations. My mother showed up at every wedding, shower, christening, birthday or retirement party to which she was invited until she couldn't manage it anymore. Even then, she'd write checks and mail cards to let nieces or nephews know she remembered them with love. Unfortunately, that connection died with her. My sister, although she lives near many of them, has little contact with our cousins and their families, and I, half a continent away, have virtually none. That's a shame. It's a story repeated by almost everyone I know. Living near your relatives isn't all that common anymore. Families may gather on holidays, for major celebrations or funerals, but getting everybody together is rare.

What and who we call family these days has shifted significantly since my childhood in the fifties. Only about a quarter of the American population lives in what we call a traditional household with a husband, wife, and minor children. When the divorce rate soared in the 1970's and '80's, patterns shifted radically. Now virtually every neighborhood has couples with multiple marriages to their credit and his, hers, and our children, a gay or lesbian couple or two, single occupant dwellings, multi-generational households, mixed race families, and so on. The face of America, the great melting pot, is changing again as new kinds of immigrants from Latin America and Asia stir the mix.

The same thing is happening in other parts of the world with freer borders, especially the European Union. Last year when I visited Edinburgh, Scotland, I noticed many more languages being spoken on the streets and a much more diverse look to the city population than when I had last visited just a couple of years earlier. On the other hand, in relatively homogeneous countries like the Balkans and certain African nations, tribal, ethnic, and religious differences are still causing wars and resurrecting old wounds. The melting pot, when it works, is highly preferable. "Red and yellow, black and white, they are precious in his sight", the old child's hymn goes, "Jesus loves the little children of the world." Why is it so hard for the rest of us?

With all the demographic and cultural shifts of the past half century, in ever increasing numbers we live separately from our families, don't know our neighbors, are largely urban populations, and no longer claim a particular religion or identity defined by what we belong to. Those whose identities used to be tied to traditional systems aligned according to family, tribe, school, religion, corporation or political party—systems they may have had no part in creating but sustained by their presence or beliefs—may suffer identity loss.

On the one hand, these changes present opportunities for people to recreate themselves free of system-imposed limits and boundaries. If you are spiritually connected and know that you are part of an interconnected set of ever-widening and -complex systems you influence and in turn are influenced by, you'll identify with the whole system, rather than seeing only the smaller parts which feel separate from everything else. The entire organic whole becomes the source of your primary identity, and you want to see the whole remain healthy and expanding and life-giving. However, if you are not spiritually connected, as you disconnect from traditional systems you can become a threat not only to yourself but also to others, a kind of outlaw or maverick who tests the limits of a newfound freedom.

The real threat presented by the 2012 scenarios we talked about earlier is the nightmare version of anarchy and lawlessness: people hoarding, panicking, pillaging, and exhibiting the worst of human behavior in the absence of any authority outside themselves. That is why it is so important for the Great Shift to happen before or as the traditional systems break down or severe Earth changes occur. In this critical moment of transformation, the answer to the question "Who is my neighbor?" is everyone and everything without exception. We love even the dark in order to bring it into the light, including the darkness within ourselves.

When you begin to design or seek an intentional community, start with the qualities and values you want to cultivate in yourself and the others who will be your primary community. Think of this particular community not in isolation but as part of an interconnected web of all other intentional communities that seek relationship throughout the universe.

While we don't know what will emerge on the other side of the Great Shift, these new communities will represent the higher consciousness. They will fulfill our needs, accommodate our creativity, support our dreams and become sustainable through our choices and practices. They'll include not only people of all types and persuasions, but also animals, birds, plants and trees, bodies of water—our entire natural world. In addition, we may become aware of realms not even in our awareness at this point. Beings in other dimensions may be more visible or present as we move into higher realms of consciousness ourselves. Many can see or feel their presences now, and more will after the shift. It's time to expand our thinking beyond the limits of the old belief systems and begin to manifest the kinds of communities we have longed to be a part of and in which we will feel not only secure, supported, and loved, as in the best of human families, but also fulfilled and expanded to the greatest possible degree as expressions of Divine Love and Light.

To prepare for this part of the shift, we can begin creating our ideal communities through our thoughts and intentions. The more energy we put behind these, the more likely and the sooner they are to manifest. We will begin to attract to ourselves the people, resources and circumstances which will fulfill our intentions and can co-create with them and with Spirit the communities we desire.

Sustainable Community

Now that you have a sense of intentional community, we'll focus on the other essential element of your community: its sustainability. The word "sustainable" is one you hear and see often these days, when people are becoming more conscious of the urgency of the human condition and that of the other species that form our complex ecosystems in the face of potential shortages and limitations of vital resources. Having a sustainable water supply, a sustainable source of energy or food, a sustainable agriculture, sustainable design, even sustainable development, which currently seems an oxymoron, means that the condition or source is renewable, replenishable, indefinitely productive, not limited by lack of resources. Let it be said that we don't really know what is sustainable and what isn't, but we are developing better techniques and tools for measuring how what we use impacts the Earth.

The Earth's "carrying capacity" is another term commonly used, primarily referring to the total numbers of beings, including the human, which Earth is capable of sustaining. The more we consume, the fewer people and other species can be accommodated. Since consumption is everywhere on the rise and the world population of just humans is approaching 7 billion, it doesn't take a mathematician to figure out we're going in the wrong direction.

In my own area, life as we know it, with unlimited uses of water for households and industries, is clearly not sustainable. Yet North Carolina, with its temperate climate, beaches and mountains, reasonable cost of living, good schools, universities, medical care, and business-friendly environment, is attracting tens of thousands more people each year than are leaving. Even if we could run pipes in from the ocean over a hundred miles away and build gigantic desalination plants to make the water potable, we'd be faced with unsustainable costs and run smack up against other needs for that water.

We can't rob Peter to pay Paul, although the federal government doesn't seem to have figured that out. Nor, by the size of our credit card debt in this country, have we. Our lifestyles clearly must change and become more sustainable if we are to survive beyond the next two generations. We can no longer continue to deplete resources and use more than our fair share. So when we contemplate the building of a sustainable community, we must consider how that community can survive and thrive on its available resources indefinitely without drawing upon the resources that belong to other regions and future generations. That's a tall order, but it's time—past time—to get started.

Finding out what resources are available in your region would be a good place to start, as you get to know your own ecosystem and its watershed. When native peoples settled in one place or another, they chose wisely through their own knowledge of the land and its fertility, the availability of an abundant supply of water and wildlife, a tolerable climate, and so on—in short, whether their community could be sustained in that place. If it could be, they stayed. If not, they moved on. When the first non-native peoples discovered America (centuries before Columbus), it's no wonder they saw this continent as a dream come true, with its abundant land, forests, rivers, wildlife, and all that could sustain them and thousands more into the future. Mostly Europeans, although the Chinese came too in the fourteenth century, they sought abundant resources which on their own continent had already been exploited and used up to the limits of their technology. Most wars in history have been fought over resources, not ideology. Ideology is used only to cover up and justify war. Witness the wars in the Middle East in our own time. Once our voracious appetite for natural resources is unleashed, it's virtually impossible to pull back.

When I drive (in my Toyota Prius, which gets 45 miles per gallon), I often listen to books on CD. The one I'm currently listening to is set in 1943, which just so happens to be the year of my birth. It's about an Irish-American Catholic family, especially three young adult girls whose love lives are impacted by the war. Listening to how the family believed in the war effort and sacrificed to support "our boys" fighting overseas by creating victory gardens (which my husband remembers well), sticking to their food rationings, wearing hand-me-down clothes, and doing without the modern conveniences we consider essential made me wonder what it would take for this and other countries to make these kinds of sacrifices and more for the sake of future generations on this planet.

What would it take for us to reduce meat consumption so that the world's grains could feed the hungry instead of animals eaten by the wealthy? Would we be willing to off load the electric grid by shutting down our part of that for several hours each day, as our family who lives in Nepal has to do? Could we eliminate our cars and downsize our houses, move closer to our work and use public transportation? Or would that seem too big a sacrifice for what might become a more sustainable lifestyle? Would we take in boarders so that not so many houses would be needed? Live in denser neighborhoods with more open land for recreation and wildlife, as new urbanists like our architect daughter recommend? What are we willing to do voluntarily before we are forced by necessity to cut back and cut off our voracious patterns of consumption?

Years ago I was part of a national faith-based organization focused on environmental stewardship. One of its projects involved raising the consciousness of churches about sustainability through "greening" congregations. In this context, green means environmentally aware and friendly. Taking simple steps like recycling church bulletins and other waste, conserving fuel, and creating awareness through activities and education for all ages significantly reduced the participating congregations' imprint on the environment. This environmental stewardship movement has grown within faith-based communities. Doing significant work in this arena is Interfaith Power and Light, a part of the Regeneration Project (www.theregenerationproject.org).

In the same way, greening our homes, schools, businesses, and hospitals can have a huge positive impact. Check to see if the institutions you're connected with are reducing, reusing, and recycling, and, if not, get a group together and start making an effort yourself. All of us must take responsibility for turning around our voracious consumption of resources.

No matter whether it's global warming and/or something else that is causing the Earth to change, we must adjust our thinking and take appropriate action as a global community to live lightly on the Earth.

One important global organization whose advocacy for the sustainability of the planet provides a framework for governments, communities, and individuals is the Earth Charter Initiative. Go to www.earthcharter.org and read the Charter. It's an amazing document, a "declaration of fundamental principles," as the website says, "for building a just, sustainable, and peaceful global society for the 21st century." Its history over the past sixteen or more years has been enlightening. First drafted for the United Nations Earth Summit of 1992, after many iterations and much effort by hundreds of organizations and international agencies throughout the world, with leadership from people like Maurice Strong, the Secretary-General of the Earth Summit, and Mikhail Gorbachev, the former Soviet Premier, consensus was finally reached on the document's principles and language in 2000. Since then the document has been widely endorsed. In its final form the Charter provides a blueprint for any community that wants to live sustainably, however large or small.

When you visit the Earth Charter Initiative's website, you may choose to endorse the document and join with millions around the world who are hoping for the transformational change this Charter represents. You can also download a free book, *The Earth Charter in Action*, and may use it to lead a class or teach your community about the principles of the Charter and how to put them into action. I strongly recommend this valuable document that represents the hopes and dreams of humanity for a sustainable future. Its four broad commitments are as follows:

1. Respect Earth and life in all its diversity.
2. Care for the community of life with understanding, compassion, and love.
3. Build democratic societies that are just, participatory, sustainable, and peaceful.
4. Secure Earth's bounty and beauty for future generations.

Community Models

As you begin to think about creating an intentional, sustainable future, having a blueprint like the Earth Charter to guide you will be extremely helpful. You may also wish to explore other good resources, such as the renowned Findhorn Community in Scotland and others like it.

Findhorn, located in northeastern Scotland not far from Inverness, began in 1962 with a handful of people whose intention was to create a spiritually focused, sustainable community. It has grown over the past decades into a model of how to build intentional, sustainable and, in this case, international community. People come from all over the world to spend time there, to take one of Findhorn's many workshops on creating and living in an ecovillage, sustainable practices, and leadership, as well as to share knowledge and experience. Like any good intentional community, Findhorn has a statement of values to which its members subscribe. They cover the following fourteen topics: Spiritual Practice, Service, Personal Growth, Personal Integrity, Respecting Others, Direct Communication, Reflection, Responsibility, Nonviolence, Perspective, Cooperation, Resolution, Agreements, and Commitment. Details may be found on their website, www.findhorn.org. Note that Spiritual Practice comes first. Their values statement about that is "I commit myself to active spiritual practice and to align with spirit to work for the greatest good." Not a bad place for any intentional community to begin. A sense of shared values is essential. Within traditional communities those typically were derived from the dominant religious, civil, or cultural beliefs and values. With the breakdown of traditional systems, people's values do not any longer necessarily conform, even within close-knit communities. Witness the generation gap in families, which virtually all of us have experienced.

Communities sharing common values that are uplifting, spiritually-based, and operate for the highest good of all, including other species, are rare and for that reason all the more valuable. Monastic communities come to mind, although the belief systems which spawn them often impose harsh conditions on their adherents. Poverty, chastity, and obedience aren't very appealing these days when people have options. In centuries past, going into a monastery or convent was a choice preferable to the alternative for many men and women. These days, particularly in a culture like America's, so into material possessions and individual freedom, most young people—even older adults—would find it hard to survive very long in such an environment. And yet I have personally found such religious communities attractive as places to retreat, experience silence, acceptance, and hospitality, and join in communal worship and singing. The simplicity and order of the committed spiritual life affords opportunities for reflection, refreshment, and renewal, something all of us need from time to time.

Another interesting ecovillage is located in Russia. Called Rodnoe, it is one of several villages spawned by the *Ringing Cedars* (www.ringingcedars.com) series of books by Vladimir Megre, based on his experience with Anastasia, a unique woman who lives close to nature in a remote Siberian forest. This extraordinary series focuses on higher consciousness ways of living in concert with Mother Earth and is so popular in Russia that ecovillages built according to Anastasia's teachings are popping up, like Rodnoe. The *Ringing Cedars* series will offer the reader fascinating material about living close to the Earth in community.

To explore the vast variety of small ecovillages and intentional communities that exist around the world, go to www.ic.org. This site, sponsored by the Fellowship for Intentional Community, is rich with books, resources and links to nearly two thousand other sites representing individual communities. You can search for those near you or in a place you might consider moving, or just explore randomly to find out what kinds of communities exist. Usually you can learn their mission and purpose, what kind of members they have, what their facilities are like, and whether they are open or closed to new members. The open ones allow you to visit to become acquainted and stick your toe in the communal water before jumping in with both feet. A number of communities are noted on the website as "forming," which means they are more of an idea and a call for participants than an actual working community. The site lists over 1400 in the U.S. and hundreds more around the world. One unique listing is from Taiwan, which notes that its community is a leper colony. Who knew there was still such a place in the world?

Most intentional communities are started by one or two people who have an idea and possibly some land. They develop the idea and put out the call to others to join them. Often individuals can purchase lots and build homes on the land that conform to the community's vision and requirements or rent existing properties. The vision may be narrow or broad, limited by gender, sexual orientation, age, or other criteria. Many of them never go anywhere, being too quirky or picky to attract the kind of people they are hoping for. Even the best of these often fail, after the founder dies or decides to sell out or gets mad at some of the residents. When people's narrow visions and egos are involved, it's difficult to make community work. Just as divorce is all too common, so are the separations of members from the community. The issues often center on money and control. These perennial human demons must be overcome in order for communities to thrive in the post-2012 world. Even the biblical community following Pentecost, according to Acts 5, was split over the actions of Ananias and his wife Saphira, who held out some of the proceeds from the sale of their land that were supposed to be given to the community. Their punishment was death, a pretty harsh lesson that put the fear of God quite literally into the early Christians, when they were supposed to be learning to trust and rely on God.

Throughout human history, when money and power become contentious people are split. The lower emotions take over from the higher ones. Until we get beyond this kind of pettiness we will not enter the kin-dom of God.

One example of intentional, sustainable communities that have done well is the co-housing community. There are many of these around the country. They typically have land held in common, and each individual or family has its own house, either already built or built according to communal standards. These tend to be smaller than the average house, because the co-housing communities usually have common buildings that serve as gathering places for communal meals, taken several times a week or month, classes for children and adults, workshops, gardens, recreation facilities, and so on. The principle is a good one: avoid unnecessary duplication of spaces and foster community spirit and relationships. Just as many housing developments have common facilities, like pools, playgrounds, and tennis courts maintained by fees split equally among residents, co-housing communities do too. But they go one step farther and share common values and a vision for their lives together. They give up some of their personal freedom in exchange for better common areas and communal support. If a co-housing community appeals to you, you might look into it now and be a step ahead of the trend when the time comes. Of course, this kind of community has existed in the past in many forms and was quite popular among counter-culture youth in the '60's through the '80's.

If times get hard, as they are likely to for a great many people, you're going to need an extended community, and when the Great Shift happens you're going to want to be part of one for sure! So it's a win-win situation to think now about forming your community so you'll be prepared for whatever comes.

You may already be part of several intentional communities, such as the family, your neighborhood, religious organization, athletic team, club, school, college or university, alumni association, membership organization, union, political party, and so on. Some of these have common visions, mission statements, goals and objectives, qualifications for membership, rules and regulations. Others may be very loosely organized. When creating a new community, the simpler the structure, the better at this point. Figure out what the group is about, who's welcome, how to share leadership, make decisions, and handle money. Groups such as these will be fluid and organic, rather than highly organized and controlled from the top. Shared leadership and decision-making by consensus takes a learning curve for those used to being in charge or being led, but it will be well worth the time and effort to get people singing on the same page as well as out of the same hymn book. Respecting individual differences is vital, but the standard you can use for all of your communities is whether or not it serves the highest good of all concerned and of the Earth.

In addition to the kinds of organizations in which people meet face to face, you may be part of new virtual communities, similar to Facebook, Myspace, Youtube, LinkedUp or the like, where people meet on the internet and share all kinds of information, or already know each other and connect via a chat group or something of the kind. I belong to a couple such groups, since I'm on line a lot and find it much easier to communicate with people by email and internet than to play telephone tag or meet in person. Those kinds of personal contacts are desirable and necessary, but it's just much quicker to email or add a few sentences to a discussion board. When this book comes out in print, I'm going to activate a new blog, www.2012iscoming.com, so that people can communicate with me and one another about how the material in the book strikes them and share ideas and resources. We will be a kind of virtual, intentional community for however long people want to stay connected.

Groups have a natural life, sometimes short, sometimes long, and when they break up, it's because their time has passed—either that or the old personality and power issues break them up. Groups of other spiritual teachers and healers and I have come together for journeys, meetings, healing exchanges, and potlucks, but when there's no longer an energy within the group for these kinds of gatherings to continue, we just let it go. If there's not a felt need for the group to exist, then releasing it is preferable to hanging on when people are moving on to something else.

In my mother's day, people stayed connected for the long haul. Mother belonged for over fifty years to a sorority formed through her church. It had about 25 members initially, all of whom lived in the Detroit area. For decades my mother never failed to gather with her sorority each month. It was her most important community apart from the family. The women in the group became like sisters to each other, knew all of each other's history, and shared common interests. Gradually some of the women moved or drifted away, but the remainder kept on until they no longer met regularly but as they could, and then stayed in touch by phone or mail and, as they aged, finally only at Christmas or on birthdays. The deep friendships that formed never died, just evolved and changed along with the needs and interests of the members.

Such communities built on mutual respect, common experiences and love nurture people and are sorely missed in today's world. They will be recreated out of the Unity Consciousness as part of the Great Shift.

Creating Your Intentional, Sustainable Community

We've covered all kinds of communities people belong to. Now let's focus on how you might create the intentional, sustainable community you choose to live with on the way to 2012 and beyond. I already know a number of people who are starting to think about the kind of group they'd like to be part of, the people they'd like to call together, and the places they would consider that would allow for the possibility of survival in the event of the kinds of changes and scenarios outlined earlier. One international group is looking into a location above the 65th parallel, expecting a pole shift will lead to major climate change and the rising of the oceans along North and South America. Regardless of whether or not you believe that something like this will happen, you need to think now about your options and be prepared for those you consider most likely as well as those that could occur.

One kind of community would be similar to those just mentioned, based on a common vision, guidelines, the creation of a unique place and the selection of people who become a community through living out their vision and developing strong relationships with each other. These kinds of communities tend to be rare and dissolve when key people leave. They are difficult to form unless the people already know and trust each other. When people try to pool their financial resources, problems often arise. While the Great Shift in consciousness may make such communities much more common, workable, and necessary, the kind that most of us will be dealing with begins with our own core communities to which we are already committed.

Unless you are planning to walk away from the people you currently live with or they from you, they will form the core of your community. So rather than beginning with the kind of vision that informed Findhorn, for example, which is a deductive, top down approach to building community, you might begin the inductive way, from the ground up, by assessing the skills and needs of those already within your group, what else you need and go from there. Rather than choosing an ideal place in an ideal location, you may begin by making provision for staying where you are.

Staying put will be the choice most of us make on the path through 2012, unless we are nudged in another direction or it is necessary to move elsewhere. Predictions from a number of sources, scientific and spiritual, indicate that the east and west coasts of North and South America are not going to be safe from disasters of various kinds. If you are within 25 miles or so of any of these coasts you may want to seriously consider moving inland or away from these areas. Even now, in the summer of 2008, we're starting to hear about "the big one", an earthquake in the Pacific Northwest of a 9.0 magnitude that could devastate Washington, Oregon, and British Columbia. New York City, Washington, D.C. and Los Angeles are potential targets for all kinds of Earth- and human-caused disasters. What's a person to do? Moving is not easy. You will need to assess just how serious the risk is in your area and decide, with spiritual guidance, whether to go or stay.

As you think about those you'd like to include in your extended community, certain individuals may come to mind, along with skill sets you might need or qualities in those you want to attract. It's important to think this through with care, as you'll want to ensure that the people who form your community share a commitment to making it work and can bring all kinds of resources and gifts to expand what you already have. The group needs to share the same general intention to live in a community which seeks to support the highest good of all and to live in harmony with each other and the natural order.

Here's a short list of the kinds of qualities and skill sets you might look for within your community. This could be expanded considerably but will give you a working idea of what it might take to meet a wide range of the kinds of needs you'll encounter.

1. **Spiritual Leader:** someone spiritually aligned, mature, and capable of drawing people together for the common good. Training in spiritual development would be helpful but not as important as wisdom and maturity. Chose someone who has learned his or her life lessons, has an open heart and mind, and can help support and strengthen the individuals and relationships in your community, keeping the spiritual focus before the group.

2. **Visionary:** someone with creative vision who can inspire the community to dream big and co-create with Spirit the kind of community which will reflect the values, needs, and available resources of the group. Together with the spiritual leader and the community manager, this person is part of the leadership team that builds consensus within the community and helps it manifest its collective vision.

3. **Community Manager:** a person with experience in managing people by bringing out the best in them and getting them working together. The manager will also keep track of the community resources, tasks, and schedules.

4. **Master Crafts Person or Engineer:** someone who knows how things work, how to use natural materials to build and repair communal buildings, how to fix things, how to teach others his/her skills, and how to build and sustain the communal physical plant. An architect or designer who is familiar with "green" building and

can lay out the physical design of the community is also desirable, especially if the community will be designed and built from the ground up or converted from an existing space.

5. **Healer:** a person trained and gifted in several of the following: spiritual energy healing, energy medicine, naturopathic healing, the uses of medicinal herbs, plants, and essential oils, healing with crystals and stones, therapies for physical, emotional, mental, and spiritual disorders and conditions. More than one healer, one of whom is perhaps also the spiritual leader, would be helpful, especially one who knows how to draw upon natural, Earth-based remedies as well as those from other dimensions. A shaman is also a good choice. People with conventional medical training and experience would also be valuable, but their usual tools–prescriptions and surgery– may not always be available or the best approach after the shift.

6. **Teachers:** one or more teachers of various subjects are needed within the community. At least one should be for the community's children, to assure their ongoing education. Teachers of all kinds of practical skills, such as sewing, cooking, gardening, building, yoga, and so on will be needed and may overlap with other skill sets. Teachers of art, writing, and music are also valuable, to support the community's creative expression.

7. **Musician:** this person may overlap with the last category. It is very important that the community sing, chant, and play musical instruments at its communal gatherings. Music is an essential expression of the Divine and helps raise the vibration of the community. It also contributes to healing.

8. **Physical Director:** someone who will help people get and stay in good physical condition, which is essential

to community survival. She/he will organize sports, exercise classes, physical games, and other activities that build bodies and relationships.

9. **Record Keeper:** someone who will keep the community's history and memory in a variety of forms. This person may be a writer, artist, teacher, or a wise one who observes and records the ongoing life of the community.

10. **Technology Coordinator:** someone who understands technology and communications systems and will find ways to maintain communication within the community and connect to the rest of the world. This may involve traveling to find and maintain relationships with other kinds of communities.

11. **Food Coordinator:** this individual will oversee the community's food supply, gardens, nutritional needs, food preparation and storage. A nutritionist or someone with a great deal of experience in the home or work setting managing food is recommended.

12. **Residential Manager:** someone skilled in ensuring that all residents have their basic needs met and making the community housing and communal buildings and grounds comfortable and clean.

If you have these twelve roles and skill sets covered, you'll be well on your way to creating a sustainable community. You may think of other categories that are not included here. Some people will be able to cover several of these and more. In my own core community, we especially need someone like our friend Wayland, who has a wide variety of experience in engineering and craftsmanship as well as skills in food preparation and home maintenance. I'd like Wayland or someone like him on my team!

It must be said that children, the elderly and disabled, and companion and domestic animals for which you have accepted responsibility must be included in such communities. Their needs must be planned for and accommodated as you conceive of the kind of community you'd like to create. Multigenerational communities are the most natural and usually the most fun. And fun needs to be part of what you co-create, for otherwise it does not reflect the higher consciousness. Members need to choose the roles they will play and the responsibilities they will carry within the community. These may be shifted from time to time, as people want to do other things or develop new skills. Those who can't work have gifts of their own to offer, such as a sense of humor or loving presence.

Concerning animals, if you're on a farm or have some land, animals can provide dairy products, eggs, and raw materials for clothing, although in a higher consciousness community would not be killed for food. Horses and mules can provide transportation of people and goods. Nowadays many domestic animals are suffering from deprivation, as shortages of grains have increased the expense of feeding horses and cows, especially. Some misguided people are abandoning or starving their animals, a cruelty that will not be abided in the consciousness of Love, in which all will have enough.

A further word about children: the children being born today and, indeed, for the past forty years are carrying vibrations and DNA that is advanced beyond the rest of us. Known as Indigos, Crystals, or Rainbows, these children have gifts of spiritual and psychic capacity, creativity and imagination, and depth of perception which are astounding. They are the amazing human beings we are beginning as a species to become, the next step in the evolutionary chain.

Indigos were the earliest of these new generations of children. They didn't fit the mold the systems they encountered tried to fit them into, and many experienced intense energies and overwhelming sensory perception they treated by self-medicating or withdrawing from the world. They are highly intuitive, very creative, and technologically innovative and advanced. Look at all the new millionaires among the twenty- and thirty-somethings, and you're likely looking at Indigo children, so named for the color associated with the third eye or psychic center of the Chakra system, which tends to dominate their auras, the egg-shaped energy fields around their bodies which some can see. Not all of that generation were Indigos, but they have seeded the planet and have been around long enough to have children.

Crystal children started appearing around the turn of the 21st century. They are brilliant and multi-faceted like crystals, creative, have a highly developed group consciousness and can often be identified by their soul-penetrating eyes. Rent the movie *The Last Mimzy* if you want to see what Crystal children are like. They have capacities beyond those developed so far by the human race, and, like the Indigos, are way showers to a more advanced way of being a cosmic human.

Rainbow kids are being born every day. Like the colors of the rainbow, they have it all. They are the personification of Divine Love and are little angels with very high vibration energy. To experience these three new varieties of the human race is to be awestruck by the power, wisdom, creativity, and love of the Creator and of these children themselves. You want to be sure that you have some of them among your communities, even in leadership roles. Age and work experience are not the most important criteria for wisdom anymore. Who said, "And a little child shall lead them"?

To begin the process of creating your community, start with your core group, then see what you've got and what you need to add to round out the skills and characteristics needed. Maybe there's someone who doesn't necessarily bring a lot of skills but has a kind, generous nature, loves everybody, and tells great stories. Such a person will enrich the lives of all. My expectation is that after the Great Shift, people who can't hold a high vibration of energy will be removed from the planet, as the whole point of this transformation is for Earth and her creatures to reflect Divine love and grace. Those who are not ready to stay will be supported in their own evolutionary processes in other realms.

Someone I know has a horse farm and is thinking about

inviting a few people to live there and co-create a new community to share resources and lives as part of being prepared for what lies ahead, as well as to participate in and anticipate the Great Shift in consciousness. The person was thinking about whom to invite and named several friends who were like-minded and compatible. I pointed out that while they were all great people they overlapped a good bit in what they would bring and that others with skills and experience to supplement this group might be needed. We tend to associate with people who share our interests and don't necessarily have the complementary qualities a whole community will need.

Another issue we will face as we begin this process of co-creation is that very few people are going to want to give up their current homes or lifestyles—at least not until they have no choice. With all the people losing their homes through foreclosure these days, that is beginning to change. But without a corresponding shift in consciousness, not many outside of their families and closest friends would want to take them in. We're going to have to get beyond our personal senses of entitlement—what we're owed or entitled to because of who we are and what we have done in our lives.

If we experience the significant Earth- and human-caused changes that would make it necessary for people to band together in small, self-sustaining communities, that will be the positive outcome of those disasters, just as every cloud has its silver lining. There is much we will have to relinquish and much we will gain. The thought of living in a community that uses group spiritual discernment to make decisions instead of doing your own thing may not be particularly appealing. Yet we'll be fortunate if we are able to choose to create the kind of community I've been describing as intentional and sustainable and if that community has access to the basic necessities of water, food, and shelter.

The new consciousness will bring with it many advantages that will make up for the things we feel attached to and don't want to give up. Imagine how the pioneers felt leaving their familiar surroundings behind and heading into unknown lands where they would face many hardships before they developed the kinds of lives they dreamed of. In the American frontier, towns grew up when people came together to provide education for their children, churches for their spiritual lives, general stores for local commerce, and law enforcement for safety and security. This enterprising spirit is what characterized the America founded on freedom from tyranny and unlimited opportunity. Even now people from all over the world want to come here for a piece of the American Dream. The dark side of that dream brought devastation to the land and its native peoples, the exploitation of slave labor, and concentration of wealth and power into the hands of the few.

The Great Shift in consciousness promises a new dream for all people, not a nightmare. Regardless of what happens to us and the Earth physically, we may have another chance at a new creation where life is abundant once and for all. We can give up a few creature comforts temporarily for that dream, that opportunity. And so I look forward with hope, not dread, trusting that Spirit will sustain us, for that is the kind of sustainability that supersedes all else.

Now is the time to begin, before we are faced with immediate crisis and emergency situations, to think about who, what, how, when, and where you'll create the community of which you will become part. I've talked about you and your community as though you were somehow isolated from all others. That will not necessarily be the case, although it could be at least temporarily. As you know, we are part of an interconnected web of creation—ecovillage within ecosystem, ecosystem within planet, planet within solar system, solar system within galaxies and star systems within the cosmos, all within One, all emanations of Divine Love. Your community or ecovillage will be a reflection of all and a generator of more, so as you create the kind of world you want to live in, remember our interconnections through all dimensions of time and space.

Trust that you will be led to the people and place that is right for you. Life in small villages interconnected by choice and mutual support could be a very appealing, satisfying way to live. Some will travel from one ecovillage to another, taking information, news, goods and resources, bringing these around the area and gathering more to take back home. Bards of old used to memorize ballads full of stories and history and travel around presenting these as entertainment as well as imparting a cultural tradition. Maybe they will again. Those of us who live through the shift will have plenty of tales of our own to tell and to transmit to future generations.

Part of your community's responsibility and desire will be to connect with others and establish wider circles of support and sharing of ideas and resources. If communications systems do not break down, that will be easier than if they do. In ancient times in Great Britain, as among native tribes in other regions, communications from one tribe or community to another was done with drumming and other vibratory instruments and signal fires. In Britain, the Celts would light hilltop fires on the four major festivals, Samhain, Imbolc, Beltane, and Lughnasadh, that signaled the changing of the season and the continuity of time, which they saw as circular, not linear. It circled around the year, from harvest to the fallow time to the time of planting and of bringing forth, the oldest cycle of the Earth giving forth her abundance to sustain all her species. The high fires helped friends, families, and towns at a distance stay connected and celebrate together their attunement with Mother Nature's promise and fulfillment.

Now few of us even notice the passing of the seasons except for changes in the weather, at least in some climate zones. When we can eat Chilean blueberries in January we get out of sync with the rhythms of the natural order, and that is what has happened. We have forgotten our roots and Earth connections, and now it's time for Mother Nature to call us back to a more natural way of being in the world. Whether the extreme changes we've talked about happen or not, it would be good for us to intentionally create and experience the more harmonious kind of existence we have forgotten. That's not to idealize the past. Rather, it's to carry forward into the future everything we have learned to create a more viable future—if it's not too late. If it is too late for this planet, this jewel of the solar system, then we shall mourn our Earth from distant star systems where we've gone to start over. Let's make the shift in time. So much is at stake.

CHAPTER NINE: DEVELOP YOUR ACTION PLAN

Whatever happens on Planet Earth on the way to 2012 and beyond is already unfolding. The particulars cannot be fully known at this time, but as we saw early on possibilities either fall away or become probabilities. The parts all of us play from here on influence the outcome. As we use our discernment and spiritual guidance to look closely at the probabilities for Earth's future and ours, we will begin to respond to these through our own preparation on many levels, which has been the focus of this book thus far. Having thought through all that we've covered, you are now ready to formulate your own action plan, your own response to the probabilities as you envision them. All we can do at this point is assess the situation and be ready to the best of our understanding and capability for the changes which lie ahead. The preparation of an action plan helps reduce fear and stress in the midst of chaos, and reducing fear is an essential part of the Great Shift. Relying on our strong spiritual connections and the communities we have built, we will face the future with hope and trust in the highest possible outcome and the greatest good for all.

Having said that, it's time to get our communities together and start formulating plans. Remember the company that was specializing in disaster preparedness plans and wanted to build a center in northern Michigan? They were going to do for you what you can do for yourselves after reading this book and reflecting on what you'll need in the event of a number of kinds of situations that may arise. Whether or not these situations are connected to the Great Shift and 2012, there are plenty of tornados, hurricanes, fires, floods, droughts, diseases, shortages of critical supplies, and other phenomena going on every day all over the world for people to concern themselves with and prepare for. This chapter will summarize what we've talked about earlier and add other suggestions for your action plan.

During the Epiphany Weekend conversation, one woman in the group strongly suggested that people start taking action rather than just talking about what might be coming. When these events happen, there's usually not a great deal of warning. People get unnerved and can't focus on what to do and where to go if they need to leave their homes. So the first step in your action plan will be to list the kinds of probabilities you want to prepare for and what will be required for each. You may ask your local authority if they have a disaster preparedness plan in place you can look at to get some ideas.

Evacuation Plan

Whether you are able to stay in your current home or have to leave temporarily or permanently, you'll need the basics: water, food, essential medicines, shelter, access to money or items to trade, and means of communication and transportation for all those in your core community, whether it's your family, companion animals, or you alone. In the latter case, your plan should include who you would hook up with as well as where and how you would meet, as going it on your own is not advisable.

In case of emergencies I've recommended before a 25-pound backpack like my cousin Carl's prepared for each person in the household or who is part of your core community. Carl's list is in Appendix A. You can amend it based on your needs. Equip your backpacks for at least two weeks of basic supplies and store them somewhere where you can grab them easily and go. You don't need a lot of changes of clothing. Make your pack something you could throw on your back or in the trunk of your car on a moment's notice if need be. Children these days are used to carrying backpacks loaded with books and lunches to school and back, so they can help you prepare a spare pack for themselves that they can handle. Be sure to include a favorite book or toy to provide comfort in unsettling circumstances and unfamiliar surroundings. Your dogs, cats, birds, and other pets will need their own provision packs, with food, meds, leashes and toys. You may also need their bedding, crates or cages. Cats like being in small carrying cases, and you'll need disposable kitty litters for them. Make sure everyone in the household and your core community has full identification in case of separation, injury, or death. Include all your contact information as well as key emergency contacts in other locations and carry this information on your person. Pets need their ID and vaccination tags on their collars. While I'm not usually in favor of microchipping pets because of the risk of tumors, some of you may choose to do this. It assumes, however, that the person who finds your pet will have access to a chip reader—not very likely in an emergency.

In addition to your backpacks, create a list of other items you would want to take if there was time to gather them or room for them in your vehicle, if any. Pack as compactly and with as much forethought as possible, remembering the experience people had in Hurricane Katrina, when the last to go had to board busses without their pets and belongings. That's no way to have to leave and start over somewhere else. Important papers and documents, like passports, birth certificates, medical and tax records and wills should be readily available, where you can retrieve and pack them within five minutes. Be sure to get any prescriptions refilled as far ahead as your health insurance will allow or pay for an extra if need be. You don't want to leave home without these or even remain in your home without access to refills in the event of systems breakdowns.

If you do need to leave home, identify a place to travel to within one full tank of gas, assuming you can drive. Factor in long lines of traffic in case everyone tries to leave town at once, which will cut down the distance you can go. This is another reason to trade in your gas guzzler for a more fuel efficient vehicle. When you know you'll have to leave and don't have someone you can stay with in another area, call to book a motel as soon as you know the direction in which you'll be headed, because all the rooms will be taken by the time you get there. I found this out in Katrina. I took a tent with me to camp out at the Humane Society shelter. The camp ground was too hard to secure the tent stakes, and the tent blew off me the first night I was there. After that I slept in my car because all the available motels were filled with Katrina refugees. Keep your cars gassed up fully at all times, as long as gas is available. If you can't drive, arrange with a neighbor or friend to pick you up on his or her way out of town and work on securing a place to stay in case you can't return immediately.

We talked earlier about the possibility of migration and the advisability of getting away from the east and west coasts of North and South America. Here is where you need to rely on your spiritual guidance and discernment. Have at least one other possible place lined up where you could go. This could be to stay with friends or family in an inland community or to make a permanent move to a place with better resources and prospects than where you live now. Jobs and schools are of course a consideration for a permanent move. For a temporary one, you can make do almost anywhere that offers the basics of shelter, water, food, and a supportive community.

Financial arrangements will also need to be made. If you have followed the earlier advice to pay off credit cards and build up a cash reserve, you'll be ready to go. Take with you numbers for all your financial accounts, so that you can call and arrange to draw upon them as needed—provided we're not talking about a financial collapse that closes banks and cuts off sources of credit. Depending on the kind of emergency that causes you to leave home, your credit cards, check books, and a few hundred dollars in cash may be sufficient for a few days away and the possibility your home will be intact when you return. By the way, don't leave financial documents and records that would give people access to your usernames and passwords when you leave, in case of looting. After the shift, this should no longer be an issue in our future world.

In more serious emergencies, credit cards may not work, out of town checks may not be taken, and at least $1000 in cash may be needed to pay for temporary housing, food, and provisions. You don't want to carry too much cash on you, but take a little more than you think you'll need. Some people like to collect investment grade coins in gold and silver. These are portable and universally exchangeable, but in certain kinds of emergencies they won't be accepted or you won't get change for them. A one ounce gold coin will bring around $900-$1000 on the open market these days, so who will be able to give you change for a tank of gas? Items you can barter may be more helpful—food, water, blankets, dog and cat food, paper diapers, hand tools, an extra can of gas—who knows? Use your creativity and imagine what might bring the best exchange for what you'll need.

You'll also need to figure out an emergency means of communication, whether it is cell phones (provided they work) or walkie-talkies or relaying messages through others. If you are in one location and your core community is in another when some kind of emergency situation occurs, have a plan for a time and place to meet if you get separated. This is basic for each household without exception. I remember the New York blackout in the '60's. My husband worked in mid-town Manhattan, and I was in northern New Jersey. Fortunately, I was able to watch the news about what was going on and didn't worry about his not getting home at the usual time. He finally managed to walk to Penn Station, got a bus to the Park and Ride on the other side of the Lincoln Tunnel and arrived home late that evening safe and sound. These things happen. Nowadays, cell phones would likely work in those circumstances, but in the event of the kinds of solar flares we're anticipating that could take out satellites and communication systems, we'll be back to smoke rings and telepathy. Knowing where your loved ones are and how and where to meet them will be crucial to your and their well-being in trying times. If you have an elderly family member or friend in a retirement community or nursing home, be sure you know what that institution's emergency evacuation plan is and how you'll be able to get to the person if you need to leave town.

As you can see, there's a lot to think about. Most of this pertains to leaving home suddenly. Not everyone is good at planning. If you are not and this feels a bit overwhelming, get your core community together over a period of several weeks to design the plan together. That makes the most sense anyway, as you and your household alone won't necessarily think of everything, and having others you're working with on plans will achieve a better result and give you more of a sense of security and confidence in your plan.

Plan for Staying Put

Having considered basic elements of emergency evacuation plans, the next scenario is staying put indefinitely. In this case, you're not pulling up stakes and leaving but potentially dealing with an economic collapse, physical disaster or temporary or longer shutdown of essential systems. You'll need to begin to plan for shortages of gas, food, and other staples and how to find and fund them. Again, let's start with the basics.

You've got shelter—your home—although possibly no source of heating or cooling. A backup generator is often helpful, especially in areas where the power goes out a lot, but won't do much good if you can't get gas, and one big enough to run your house will be expensive and impractical. You'll need to consider a safe source of heat. Converting a gas-log fireplace to a wood-burning one or installing a wood stove will make you more self-sufficient, although tearing down forests to heat your home is counter-productive. If it's a temporary situation, send your kids out to forage for dead branches and wood scraps that can provide some measure of heat. Wear more clothes, sleep together for warmth, shut down most of your dwelling and conserve energy. Use the heat source to cook also, things like soups and stews and some of the dehydrated foods you've stored. You can also stockpile some wood pellets or other source of fuel in a safe place that won't cause your dwelling to turn into a tinder box if it ignites by accident. Better yet, convert your home to solar or wind power if possible and live off the grid.

If you're an apartment or condo dweller or live in a development that's strict about changes to your property, have a conversation with your association about what to do in case of emergency. Encourage your homeowners' association to develop a disaster preparedness plan. Now that you know what to do, volunteer to head up the team that works on the plan. It should include some kind of neighbor-to-neighbor notification system, where you check up on each other and have a way to report in that you're okay or need help. Make sure each resident has a list of contact information for the whole neighborhood.

In some areas heating isn't so much a problem, like North Carolina in the summer. Cooling is more the issue. In the absence of air conditioning, it can be brutal here. Be sure your home has screens for the windows and doors and some kind of cross-ventilation that will keep air circulating. Ceiling fans won't help if there's no electricity. Sleeping outside on a patio or deck or in a tent where a cool breeze may be available is something past generations were used to. Now we're so used to our conveniences we imagine we can't do without them.

Certain kinds of houses are well insulated to both retain heat when it's cold and stay cool when it's hot. Check out energy-efficient technologies that will work in the absence of gas and electricity. Ensuring that your home is comfortable no matter what—or at least habitable—will be important. Hardwood, tile, and vinyl floors which can be swept are better than carpets that accumulate dirt, even mold without air conditioning and electric vacuum cleaners.

Think about how to outfit your home to work for you even in extreme conditions. If you are someone's tenant, talk over with your landlord what adaptations might be needed in the space you rent, like window screens or better insulation. Develop a good relationship with the person who owns your dwelling or with the association that manages it, so that you will be taken seriously. You may have little leverage other than to withhold part of the rent until needed changes are made. If you live in a high-rise, you may want to consider moving to a lower level or to a place where the windows can be opened.

Go low tech by substituting household items and tools which can work without electricity. Some kerosene lamps, flashlights (stock up on batteries), and other camping equipment can be useful if the power is out for any length of time.

Once your shelter is squared away, make sure you have a workable water source other than city water. If you have a well, be sure you have a means of pumping the water without electricity. Hand pumps worked just fine in the past. Incidentally, you'll need a backup water supply in addition to your well, especially in drought conditions. A friend was telling me in January that neighbors' wells in her Boone, NC mountain area were running dry. That doesn't bode well, as public water isn't available in areas like those. Rainwater and ponds are about the only alternatives. Trying to sell your property when your well runs dry isn't an option, so unless you can solve the water problem before it happens, you may be better off moving to an area with plentiful water.

Get in the habit of routinely collecting rainwater in barrels or containers. This water can be used for your gardens now and later, when water is short, for bathing or washing clothes, even for drinking, if purified. If a storm is coming through, fill up your bathtubs and basins to ensure enough water to tide you over while the power is out. Be sure to have a good filtration system in your home for city water and a portable one that can be used for rain, pond or other fresh water source for drinking. Water may be one of your biggest challenges. Even now you need a good filtration system for public water systems, which are prone to chemical pollutants or sediment you wouldn't want your family to drink. Just recently a report came out that the public water supplies in 41 American cities were laced with all kinds of medications and toxins. A reliable source of potable water is essential. Storing water in plastic containers that leach into the water isn't a great idea either for the long term. Making fresh water by using a filtration system is best, although you need a supply of potable water on hand for all in your household for several days at least, so water in plastic jugs that you use up and replace frequently is okay.

Providing a steady source of food is your next challenge. It's a good idea to stockpile some dehydrated foods, as mentioned earlier, for any kind of emergency. I noticed on Costco's website not long ago that they are selling an emergency food bucket with enough for 275 meals for $79.95. Intriguingly, they also had several other emergency provision packs, including one with food and other supplies for two for six days. The fact that these are showing up in stores where millions shop says that being prepared for unknown circumstances and disasters is in the public consciousness. That's good, because it means many more people will be ready when the time comes.

Beyond emergency provisions, consider establishing a vegetable garden. Add a few fruit trees and bushes, if possible. Apartment and condo dwellers can join together to create gardens on their grounds to supplement other food sources. In city neighborhoods, small towns, and suburban developments, neighbors are your best bet for an extended intentional, sustainable community. That begins with getting to know your neighbors well enough to have a conversation with them about what may lie ahead. If you've lived in one place long enough you probably also have friends not in your neighborhood but nearby who can become part of your community. Start thinking now about who you'd want to share the experience of preparing for the coming changes with.

We live in a new development that's only one street long with about twenty households. Within the neighborhood we have two ponds stocked with fish, so we have a fresh water source and food source which if we're careful is sustainable. Wild blackberries grow in the summer, and if we harvest and preserve them, they'll provide some nourishment. We've begun developing relationships with neighbors in order to be prepared for the kinds of conditions we've discussed which may necessitate our working together to help provide each other's basic needs.

Community gardens are a great way to begin your preparation, as you can benefit from them now, and it usually takes several years to fully prepare the soil so that your garden will be its most productive. A good book on gardening is Steve Solomon's *Gardening When It Counts: Growing Food in Hard Times*. Steve, a seasoned vegetable gardener and former vegetable seed company owner, tells you exactly what you'll need in any kind of conditions to grow and harvest enough vegetables to provide at least 50% of your core community's caloric needs for a year. Steve notes that during the hard times his native Britain experienced from about 1930 through World War II and beyond, families survived on their "allotments" or community garden plots. It didn't take a lot of land, but it did take people working cooperatively and smartly to ensure that these gardens provided the maximum yield possible and the nutrition needed. No exotic veggies here—just those with the highest nutritional value, like beans, peas, carrots, onions, potatoes, tomatoes, squash, melons, and so on. People got smart about not planting all their tomato plants at one time so as to have veggies ripening through the summer and fall seasons. Countries like Russia and Cuba have also allotted garden plots for residents which have provided significant food sources for them in hard times. Cuba, which has banned pesticides, produces some of the best vegetables in the world, according to Steve. I hope we get to sample some in the future.

Communal gardens become places where people gather, share the work, and enjoy the harvest mutually. If your neighborhood doesn't have one, start one as soon as possible. Canvas your neighbors to see who'd be willing to help and share the garden's produce among these, as well as those whose circumstances make participation difficult or impossible. Distribute some of the extra produce to the others as well. Maybe the following year they'll join in. Hang out at your local farmers' market and notice who produces the best home grown foods. Ask if you can help out in their fields during planting, maintaining, or harvesting to get some experience and good tips. Maybe they'll even cut you in on a share of the produce. This is a great idea for people who don't have the time or space to create much of a garden on their own. Similarly, Community Supported Agriculture (CSA) is growing in popularity. This involves developing a relationship with a local farm by buying a share in its food production and receiving fresh produce and other farm products.

It doesn't matter if you live in a place with big lots or small. If there's not much land available or a ready water source, Steve's book will teach you how to plant smartly even in drought conditions. Can't afford to buy plants grown in pots to transplant into your garden? Steve says that's not the way to go anyway. He leads you to the best, more cost-effective sources of seeds and ways to get the best yields from them. If you live in a condo or apartment community, get a few neighbors together and start a patio or rooftop garden or get your homeowners' association to allocate a part of the community land for a garden. You can even grow a few veggies or sprouts in your home, if you have good light, on a balcony or deck or in your kitchen. If you get started now you'll begin to develop the expertise and enthusiasm for growing your own food that will stand you in good stead in the future. By making it a communal effort, you'll be on your way to creating a core intentional, sustainable community.

Whether you stay put, as we're hoping to do, or are guided or forced to move to another location, you'll need the kind of basic skills just mentioned within your group: gardeners and fishers can provide most of what you need to live on, providing you have a reliable water source. Kids generally love to fish and garden and can do a lot of the grunt work while the adults focus on supervision. Having a few community cookouts and fish fries when the harvest comes in is a great idea and helps cement relationships.

Health and Wellness

Medical supplies will be an issue in the future. While I don't want to take anything away from the medical profession, its focus is on diagnosis, prescribing medications, and surgery. Unless you have a physician or nurse in your community, you won't have access to this kind of medical care unless you can travel to a place that has it. Instead, the focus needs to be on staying healthy and learning how to use natural herbs and products as well as energy healing for wellness.

After the Great Shift, it's unlikely that obesity and its related diseases like heart attacks, strokes, and diabetes will still be major health issues. The higher consciousness brings with it a sense of respect for the body and its complex systems and a desire to stay physically fit. Genetic disorders may also be a thing of the past. Natural forms of exercise will keep people in shape, like walking, foraging for mushrooms, berries, or medicinal plants, gardening, and working around the community. Our high tech forms of entertainment, like HDTV, video games, and iPods, may or may not be available, but communal entertainment will be more appealing. Active and board games, community sings and the like are a lot more fun than solitary TV-watching. The point: people won't be as sedentary as they are now. Getting outdoors in the fresh air (if there is any) and doing things with others will be a more likely pattern in our communal futures.

That being the case, we'll experience less stress and disease. So much stress currently comes from a sense of lack and having to work hard to make ends meet as well as from difficult relationships. Those of us who know spiritual energy healing and energy medicine will teach others and offer these services to each other within the community. Removing energy blocks and restoring harmonious balance to our energy fields will keep us happy, healthy, and spiritually connected. For those who do experience illness or disease, a variety of natural remedies are available. Techniques and strategies have been learned by a great many of us that will improve prospects for long and healthy lives in the future. Alternatives to allopathic medicine abound. For those of you dealing with cancer, check out Bill Henderson's website, www.beating-cancer-gently. com and buy his book on ways to approach healing cancer through strengthening the immune system, nutrition, and supplements rather than killing healthy cells along with cancerous ones through the primitive techniques of radiation and chemotherapy.

Part of what the alternative community of healers is about is educating people to know themselves at all levels—emotional, mental, and spiritual as well as physical. While some physicians understand the mind-body connection, few understand mind-body-spirit connections and have the time to treat the whole person. That's where the new wellness strategies and techniques come in which will eventually replace most of what we call medicine today. In the future we may learn how to grow new body parts or communicate with our cells to heal them before disease takes root. Meanwhile, as far as your action plans are concerned, be sure to take training yourself in one or more energy healing modalities, acquire a library of reference books and articles, stockpile some natural remedies, and take charge of your own health.

A friend had lymphoma not long ago and had her enlarged spleen, the size of a collapsed soccer ball, removed. She only weighed 110 pounds normally, so you can imagine what carrying this spleen around felt like. Instead of taking conventional medications, a couple of years ago she put herself on a macrobiotic diet, gets regular massage and exercise, and meditates. She feels great and has had no recurrence of her disease. A positive attitude and taking control of your body is essential to good health. So begin now to work on this aspect of your own life, and you'll be in good shape when the Great Shift happens. For those in your community or family who currently have serious health issues, get them started on a positive regimen in addition to what their doctors advise. It can only help and gives them a better chance of surviving the coming changes.

Communication and Transportation Systems

Just as mentioned in your emergency evacuation plan, you'll need a communications system within your community and from one location to another. If technology is working, that's easy. If not, you'll have to invent one. Having someone in your group who knows how to do this kind of work will be important. You can also designate signals—either sounds or flashing lights of some kind—if you want the community to gather at a pre-determined site. A kid on a bike or a person on a horse can also take news around, if need be. You can get inventive with systems which could work either temporarily or longer.

Mentioning bikes and horses brings up the issue of trans-portation. Today oil closed above $146 a barrel! Pump prices around here are over $4.00 a gallon. Yes, that's still cheap by European standards, but Americans and Canadians, used to driving or flying vast distances to visit people or carry out business, are having to curtail their activities and stick closer to home. Since we've already reached peak oil, we're on a slippery downward slope with regard to using cars and airplanes as our main modes of transport. Public transportation is preferable, but few communities are well set up for that. City dwellers will have the edge here, but busses and local trains will also cut back as fuel shortages occur. Alternative energy sources are still under development. Auto manufacturers seem to be betting on electric and gas hybrids as the cars of the future, yet neither power source is currently renewable, as wind and solar power are. So the likelihood is that the average community may have to rely on bikes, walking, and possibly horses and mules with carts or buggies, if food and water is available for the animals. This means that travel as we know it could be a thing of the past. I've been trying to get all my international traveling in before the cut-backs come. Businesses for years have been promoting telecommuting and reducing company travel, so this is already a trend.

Local economies, as mentioned earlier, will be the norm. A few mopeds and golf carts in your community would be usable for a while, but unless the Great Shift brings with it new kinds of technologies far advanced beyond what's currently available—which I believe will happen in time—we may be in for a post-automobile society. Imagine what a shock this is to my system, having grown up in Motown, the daughter of a Chrysler engineer! Life may not seem worth living to those who can't imagine doing without their conveniences and toys, but now is the time to get priorities straight.

The intentional, sustainable community you've created may become fairly self-sufficient in time. Whether it is or not, you'll still want to stay connected to other nearby communities to socialize and to exchange and barter goods and services. That basic economic system worked well in the past and can again. Transportation to those communities will be important, especially if other communications systems are not reliable. If you know your friends' community ten miles away has a bag of the kind of seed you need and you have a tool they want, you could meet halfway and do an exchange. If you can't communicate ahead of time, you'll have to take what you want to trade and make a deal when you get there. Visiting other communities will allow you to bring back ideas and expertise not available in your own. Cross-fertilization can make life more productive and fun.

We've looked at shelter, water and food supply, health and medications, communications, transportation, a basic economy, and the importance of community. With these covered in your action plan, I suggest that you make lists and checklists of items to purchase and stockpile, as funds and storage are available. This advice may sound like a broken record, but you don't need to prepare alone. Get your community together, even if it's a few neighbors, and start figuring out who has what, who will get what, and where it will be stored. Seeds need special handling, as do dehydrated food and stored water. The list of resources in Appendix B contains some good books with the kinds of lists you'll want, although making your own causes you to focus on getting ready and involving others.

Selling and trading or giving away what you don't need that takes up room for what you will need is something to get on top of immediately. Clean out those garages, basements, attics, closets, and storage sheds. Have a community yard sale or cart your stuff to the thrift shop or town dump. Paring down makes it easier to move quickly in another direction and is an exercise in freeing yourself from being buried by your stuff. When I wrote the *Graceful Living* book, I offered seven graceful living concepts to live by. Mentioned earlier was simplicity. Another was frugality, a lost virtue which will make a comeback in future society. Frugality denotes moderation and temperance in consumption with an eye to the common good. Both of these concepts are linked to justice and sustainability, which absolutely will be part of the Great Shift.

As you prepare your action plan, keep in mind that you're helping not only your family and core community to survive and thrive on the path through 2012 but also the entire planet. Seen from that perspective the work we do to prepare feels less like a burden and a loss and more like a net gain for the whole of creation.

That brings us to the last item I suggest you include in your action plan. It's the subject of the final chapter, "Widen the Conversation." Be sure to include how you'll spread the word to others to encourage them to understand and prepare for the Great Shift and the path to 2012 and beyond.

CHAPTER TEN: WIDEN THE CONVERSATION

Congratulations! Now that you're read this far, you're one of the better informed people on the planet about what may occur in the next few years. You are also already participating in the Great Shift to a higher consciousness by your awareness and desire to be a part of the most significant transformation on Planet Earth in the history of the human race.

Since you now know how important it is that as many people as possible become as aware as you are as quickly as possible, I encourage you to begin to widen the conversation about the topics we've covered in this book among all those whose lives you now touch—your family, neighbors, friends, co-workers, religious communities, clubs, home owners' associations, environmental groups, emergency preparedness teams, and so on. Make a list of all the people and organizations to which you will spread the word, as time is running out. The sooner more people raise their consciousness, the faster the Great Shift will occur.

Through the morphic resonance covered earlier, humanity can reach a higher vibration consciousness in time to save our species and the planet. Our hope is that all will reach this level of enlightenment before the massive Earth- and human-caused changes take place. Of course, these events in themselves will cause many survivors to open their hearts, release fear, and feel compassion for those who have suffered losses. But there are better ways to get to that place of caring and harmonizing with Divine love without going through the trauma and pain. That's why I have written this book, to help people find their way through the years leading up to 2012 and following so that they may experience the best of what is to come rather than the worst.

The choice is up to each of us. If we choose to stay on this planet and create a new world built around spiritual connection, reverence for all life and all that supports life, and co-creating loving communities which empower and enable life at a higher level than ever before, we will represent the hope for the future of this planet and the evolution and transformation of the human race. We can also choose to go through transition and assist the shift from another dimension, as many are already doing. Having experienced the transition through death of five people I cared about in the past few months, I know that several of these were being called home to help the rest of us. They completed their work here and can assist now from a higher plane. Then there are those who will choose to ignore the spiritual guidance and the evidence before us and continue business as usual, along with those who will not know what is coming. These people are not likely to survive the changes. They will experience a different future, perhaps in another realm.

Approaching the Conversation

Which do you choose? Which do you want for your own loved ones? If you choose to stay and be part of Earth's shift to higher dimension consciousness, then I urge you to begin to widen the conversation as soon as possible. Let me suggest a few ways.

At the beginning of this book I attempted to draw readers in by bringing up evidence of Earth- and human-caused changes which most people could connect to: global warming and climate change, financial crises, disasters of various kinds, and worldwide political and economic shifts. I think that's the place to start the conversation with most people. Everyone has experienced something recently which can act as a hook to interest them in hearing more.

They know these kinds of events and conditions are influencing their lives and are concerned.

In that connection, a couple of months ago I met an interesting young couple. The wife works for the Sierra Club, an organization I admire for its work in environmental protection. I mentioned this book, and she told me she's had some success working with churches to raise awareness and take action on energy conservation through organizations like Interfaith Power and Light, which has engaged over 4000 congregations thus far in studying and acting on issues of environmental stewardship. Now, ten years after I began my own similar efforts, this kind of work is bearing fruit. Partnerships between nonprofits and businesses can move the agenda of raising awareness and reducing consumption ahead far faster than individuals working alone.

The husband is finishing a Ph.D. in environmental economics, with a focus on water resources. How timely is that! I applauded both of them for their commitment. He said that he had just had a conversation with his mother in which she reflected a new understanding and awareness of the kind of issues he has been working on. It amazed him that she had been listening to him and was now able to share his concerns.

These are examples of how the conversation gets going and keeps going. People already have experienced enough extreme weather and financial crises to be concerned. They are ready to hear more and to find out what they can do to turn things around and personally prepare for what is to come. Start the conversation with today's headlines: the price of oil or gold or the latest evidence of water shortages in your area, housing foreclosures and the mortgage crisis, or whatever is already in the public consciousness. You can expand the conversation by giving other examples and encouraging people to read this book and other recommended resources to educate themselves and continue to widen the circle of those whose level of awareness is increasing. Remember, we're not looking for people to go into fear but rather to raise their consciousness about how a changing world is affecting them and what the consequences could be. This should naturally lead to the question, "What can I do?" When that happens, you'll be on your way to creating conversation partners, a study group, or an online chat group about how to find out what's going on and how to prepare for what lies ahead.

Many people are also growing in awareness about the consciousness shift. That's another way to draw them into conversation. People want to lead healthier, less stressful lives, are tired of rampant materialism and over-consumption and would welcome discussion and suggestions about how to make their own shift. More and more resources are out there on the web and in the media to assist them. Lead them to some of these and keep the conversation going.

If you feel isolated among your family and acquaintances and don't think they'd be receptive to this material, build an online group through one of the many websites which offers this opportunity. My own blog, www.2012iscoming.com, is a place to start. People can leave comments, make suggestions, list resources, and develop friendships in a kind of virtual community of support for getting ready for 2012 and the shift.

Speaking of 2012, I've treated it in this book more as a metaphor than an actual physical time for the shift to occur, but it has a literal level as well, presented earlier. People are being exposed to talk of 2012, the Mayan Calendar, and some of the prophecies and predictions mentioned here. They will want to know more. Again, this book and some of the other resources listed in Appendix B will fill them in.

As you begin to create your intentional, sustainable community, you will carry on many conversations with the people you'd like to include in your group. You can meet monthly for a study of the materials in this book, read up on intentional communities and living sustainably in more detail, and possibly make group visits to a few ecovillages and similar communities that intrigue you. As you begin to make these connections, arrangements, and preparations, you'll be widening the circle of those who are in the know and, as you tell others what you're doing, they'll be curious and can be given an opportunity to participate.

Take Positive Action

Just as nonprofits are getting together to develop strategies for responsible stewardship of the environment, this subject can become a topic of conversation in your household, work places, and organizations. If you see wasteful practices, come up with useful alternatives. Look into responsible waste disposal, too, because the obsolete electronics we all possess—computers, cell phones, ink cartridges and the like—need to be disposed of in ways that protect the environment. Show those who are a part of your life your own commitment to caring for the creation, the beloved Earth we are privileged to call home, and they may deepen their own involvement by taking beginning steps to change patterns of consumption and waste disposal.

There are so many ways in which you can make a difference. As you begin to think about these, ask your spiritual guidance to show you more, and act upon them. Involve others every step of the way. If you have children, give them roles they can play. One can be responsible for seeing that at home and at school everything possible gets recycled. Another can ensure that lights and electronic equipment are turned off when not in use. One can read labels on food products and get interested in nutrition and healthful cooking. Another can take responsibility for starting the family garden and distributing produce to the neighbors.

You'll need to keep yourself informed about the issues and solutions, so join some of the organizations listed in Appendix B, like Interfaith Power and Light, the Sierra Club, the Earth Charter Initiative, the Humane Society of the US, the Center for the New American Dream, and the Institute of Noetic Sciences, depending on your interests. These organizations and others like them have educational programs and action-oriented options for your participation. You can create your own organization with the people you bring into the conversation, with regular meetings or online communications, lists of resources, suggested tips and strategies, and so on. Start your own blog and invite everyone you know to participate. The options are limitless as long as we still have access to the means of communication we currently enjoy. Again, time is short and acting on your own commitment is paramount.

I hope I have impressed upon you the urgency of our common work. Encourage others to read this book, if you have found it helpful, and direct them to sites where they can acquire other resources to help them choose a new way of living and begin to manifest it now.

We live in exciting times! Stay hopeful and heart-centered and take positive action individually and with your communities. Universal wisdom and love will guide us each step of the way, so whatever happens on the path through 2012, trust that it will be ultimately for the highest good of all.

As we begin to shape our own paths into the future and connect our energy with positive intention, our collective high vibration will lift, shift, and transform Earth, our home, into a place of endless peace, joy, creativity and love. I send you much love and light and many blessings on your way!

APPENDIX A: CARL'S 25-POUND BACKPACK

B elow are the carefully researched and organized contents of my cousin Carl's two-week survival backpack. Most brand names are not given but are readily available from companies like REI and Go Gear. This equipment should last one person up to two weeks, provided additional water is available.

Pack Weight	Pounds/Ounces
Core total (backpack, tarp w/8 stakes, ground cloth/ space blanket, sleeping pad/insulated mat or sleeping bag, 50'/25' rope)	5/10
Extra clothes total (hiking socks, T-shirt, Army Polypropylene sleeping shirt, long underwear, Doo rag,Poly gloves, bandana, fleece hat, rain suit, shell jacket)	2/9.6
Survival total (first aid kit, head lamp, water filter, compass, map, duct tape, Leatherman micro knife + tools)	1/8
Housekeeping/kitchen total (cook kit, stove, fuel canister, wind screen, spork, toilet paper, hand sanitizer, toothbrush and powder, 2 camp towels, 64 oz. water bladder*, collapsible water bucket)	2/10.5
Total	12/4
Miscellaneous (blow-up pillow, pills, matches, 1/6 plastic bags, mosquito hat and repellant)	1/6
Food (instant oatmeal, protein bars, Myoplex powder, Gatorade powder, Emergen-C, Pack-Lite Foods, Cup-a-Soup, instant potatoes, protein powder, Crystal Lite packets, Gorp (1/4 c. each cashews, dried cherries, sour Gummy Bears, M&Ms))	11/0
Grand Total	25 pounds
*64 oz. water bladder when full	4/9

APPENDIX B: LIST OF RESOURCES

Books

Adam. *The Path of the Dreamhealer: The Quantum World of Energy Healing.* Toronto, Ontario: Viking Canada, 2006.

Berry, Thomas. *The Dream of the Earth.* San Francisco, CA: Sierra Club Books, 1990.

Brown, Dan. *The Da Vinci Code.* New York: Doubleday, 2003.

Calleman, Carl. *The Mayan Calendar and the Transformation of Consciousness.* Rochester, VT: Bear & Co., 2004.

Capra, Fritjof. *The Web of Life: A New Scientific Understanding of Living Systems.* New York, NY: Anchor Books, Doubleday, 1996.

_____. *The Hidden Connections: Integrating the Biological, Cognitive, and Social Dimensions of Life into a Science of stainability.* New York: Doubleday, 2002.

Clark, Hulda Regehr. *The Cure for All Diseases.* Chula Vista, CA: New Century Press, 1995.

Clow, Barbara Hand. *The Mayan Code: Time Acceleration and Awakening the World Mind.* Rochester, VT: Bear & Co., 2007.

Daly, Herman E. and John B. Cobb, Jr. *For the Common Good: Redirecting the Economy Toward Community, the Environment, and a Sustainable Future.* Boston: Beacon Press, 1994.

Dunham, Laura. *Graceful Living: Your Faith, Values, and Money in Changing Times.* RCA Printing, 2002. Available at www.healingandwisdom.com.

Eden, Donna with David Feinstein. *Energy Medicine.* New York, NY: Penguin Putnam, 1999. Rev. Ed., 2008.

Gore, Al. *Earth in the Balance: Ecology and the Human Spirit.* New York, NY: Plume Penguin, 1993.

Gottlieb, Bill. *Alternative Cures: The Most Effective Natural Home Remedies for 160 Health Problems. Emmaus, PA:* Rodale, 2002.

Gray, Martin. *Sacred Earth: Places of Peace and Power.* New York, NY: Sterling Publishing, 2007.

Green, Glenda. *Love Without End: Jesus Speaks.* Sedona, AZ: Spiritus Publishing, Rev. Ed., 2006.

Hawken, Paul, Amory Lovins, and L. Hunter Lovins. *Natural Capitalism: Creating the Next Industrial Revolution.* New York: Little, Brown and Co., 1999.

Henderson, Bill. *Cancer-Free: Your Guide to Gentle, Non-toxic Healing (2nd edition).* Booklocker.com, Inc., 2007

Hicks, Esther and Jerry. *Ask and It is Given: Learning to Manifest Your Desires.* Carlsbad, CA: Hay House, 2004.

Hubbard, Barbara Marx. *The Revelation: Our Crisis is a Birth.* Sonoma, CA: The Foundation for Conscious Evolution, 1993.

Jang, Hwee-Yong. *The Gaia Project 2012: The Earth's Coming Great Changes.* Trans. Mira Tyson. Woodbury, MN: Llewellyn Publications, 2007.

Kingsolver, Barbara with Steven L. Hopp and Camille Kingsolver. *Animal, Vegetable, Miracle: A Year of Food Life.* New York, NY: HarperCollins Publishers, 2007.

Lipton, Bruce. *The Biology of Belief: Unleashing the Power of*

Consciousness, Matters, & Miracles. Santa Rosa, CA: Mountain of Love/Elite Books, 2005.

McTaggart, Lynne. *The Intention Experiment.* London, England: HarperElement, 2007.

Megre, Vladimir. *The Ringing Cedars Series, Books 1-9.* New York, NY: Ringing Cedars Press, 2004-2008.

Myss, Carolyn and C. Norman Shealy, M.D. *The Creation of Health: The Emotional, Psychological, and Spiritual Responses That Promote Health and Healing.* New York, NY: Random House, 1993.

Myss, Carolyn. *Why People Don't Heal and How They Can.* New York: Crown Publishing Group, 1998.

Nearing, Helen and Scott. *The Good Life: Helen and Scott Nearing's Sixty Years of Self-Sufficient Living.* New York, NY: chocken Books, 1979.

Radin, Dean. *Entangled Minds: Extrasensory Experiences in a Quantum Reality.* New York, NY: Paraview Pocket Books, 2006.

Rasmussen, Larry L. *Earth Community Earth Ethics.* Maryknoll, NY: Orbis Books, 1996.

Schumacher, E.F. Small is Beautiful: Economics as if People Mattered. New York, NY: HarperPerennial, 1973.

Sheldrake, Rupert. *Dogs That Know When Their Owners Are Coming Home.* New York, NY: Three Rivers Press, 1999.

Singer, Peter. *Writings on an Ethical Life.* New York: The Ecco Press, 2001.

Smith, Andrew. *The Revolution of 2012, Vol. 1: The Preparation.* Glastonbury, England: Ford-Evans Publishing, 2006.

Solomon, Steve. *Gardening When It Counts: Growing Food in Hard Times.* Gabriola Island, BC, Canada: New Society Publishers, 2005.

Sounds True, ed. *Mysteries of 2012: Predictions, Prophecies & Possibilities.* Boulder, CO:Sounds True, Inc., 2007.

Stein, Matthew. *When Technology Fails: A Manual for Self-Reliance & Planetary Survival.* White River Junction, VT: Chelsea Green Publishing, 2000.

Steingraber, Sandra. *Living Downstream: A Scientist's Personal Investigation of Cancer And the Environment.* New York, NY: Vintage Books, 1998.

Swimme, Brian and Thomas Berry. *The Universe Story: From the Primordial Flaring Forth to the Ecozoic Era—A Celebration of the Unfolding of the Cosmos.* San Francisco, CA: HarperSanFrancisco, 1994.

Targ, Russell and Jane Katra. *Miracles of Mind: Exploring Nonlocal Consciousness and Spiritual Healing.* Novato, CA: New World Publishing, 1999.

Weisman, Alan. *The World Without Us.* New York, NY: Thomas Dunne Books, 2007.

Wilson, E.O. *The Future of Life.* New York: Alfred A. Knopf, 2002.

_____. *The Creation: An Appeal to Save Life on Earth.* New York: W.W. Norton & Co., 2006.

Winter, Mick. *Peak Oil Prep: Three Things You Can Do to Prepare for Peak Oil, Climate Change and Economic Collapse.* Napa, CA: Westsong Publishing, 2006.

Young, D. Gary. *Essential Oils Integrative Medical Guide.* Essential Science Publishing, 2003.

Movies/DVDs

Note: All listed below are available as DVDs through www.amazon. com and www.blockbuster.com and other outlets except *Mindwalk*, available through www.half.com in VHS format.

2001: A Space Odyssey
An Inconvenient Truth
Mindwalk
The China Syndrome
The Last Mimzy
The Milagro Beanfield War
The Secret
What the Bleep?!—Down the Rabbit Hole

Organizations and Businesses

American Society for the Prevention of Cruelty to Animals, www. aspca.org
AMORC, Rosicrucian Order, www.rosicrucian.org
Association for Research and Enlightenment, www.edgarcayce.org
Biodynamic Farming and Gardening Association, www.biodynamics. com
Center for a New American Dream, www.newdream.org
Earth Charter Initiative, www.earthcharter.org
Findhorn Foundation, www.findhorn.org
Humane Society of the US, www.hsus.org
Institute of Noetic Sciences (IONS), www.ions.org
Interfaith Power and Light & The Regeneration Project, www. theregenerationproject.org
Lehman's, www.lehmans.com
Sierra Club, www.sierraclub.org
The Foundation for International Community Assistance, www. villagebanking.org
The Heifer Project, www.heifer.org
Whidbey Institute for Earth, Spirit, and Community, www.

whidbeyinstitute.org
Wild Earth Nepal, www.wildearthnepal.com

Websites and Blogs

Barbara Hand Clow, www.handclow2012.com
Donna Eden, www.innersource.net
Barbara Marciniak, www.pleiadians.com
Barbara Marx Hubbard, www.barbaramarxhubbard.com
Bill Henderson, www.beating-cancer-gently.com
Carl Calleman, www.calleman.com
Hummingbird Living School, www.hummingbirdlivingschool.com
Intentional Communities,www.ic.org
Laura Dunham, www.healingandwisdom.com, www.2012iscoming.com
Mitch Batros' Earth Changes Media, www.earthchangesmedia.com
The Oneness Movement, www.onenessmovement.org
The Rev. Maria Nartoomid, www.spiritmythos.org
The Rev. Terri Newlon, www.terrinewlon.com
Tom Kenyon, www.tomkenyon.com

ABOUT THE AUTHOR

Laura Dunham has had three interesting careers: higher education, financial planning, and ministry. In the first, she taught English, published books, and served as an academic dean and vice president. She also served on the boards of a college and a national nonprofit. In the second, she counseled hundreds of clients, wrote a weekly newspaper column, appeared frequently in media like *Money Magazine, The Wall St. Journal,* and *U.S. News & World Report* and consulted for organizations. In the third, she served as a pastor of churches and a governing body administrator. Her specialties in ministry were financial and environmental stewardship, mission, and spiritual development. She was a trustee of a national church-related foundation for seven years and was commissioned by the Ecumenical Stewardship Center to write *Graceful Living: Your Faith, Values, and Money in Changing Times,* published in 2002.

In addition to B.A., M.A., M.Div., and Ph.D. degrees, Laura holds a Certificate in Spiritual Formation. She was a Certified Financial Planner for twenty-one years and for a time co-chaired the board of the New Mexico Community Foundation.

Following an early retirement, Laura moved to Chapel Hill, NC with husband, Alden, son, Tom, and their companion animals. She opened a center where she taught spiritual development, metaphysics, and spiritual energy healing for people, places, and the planet. Her work and interests have taken her to more than forty countries around the world. She now focuses on sharing through her writing her spiritual journey and the knowledge, experience, and wisdom it has brought her over her lifetime.